SKETCH MAP OF THE
MIDLAND MAIN LINE BETWEEN
LONDON (ST PANCRAS) AND DERBY

All station names shown are the original ones.

NOT TO SCALE

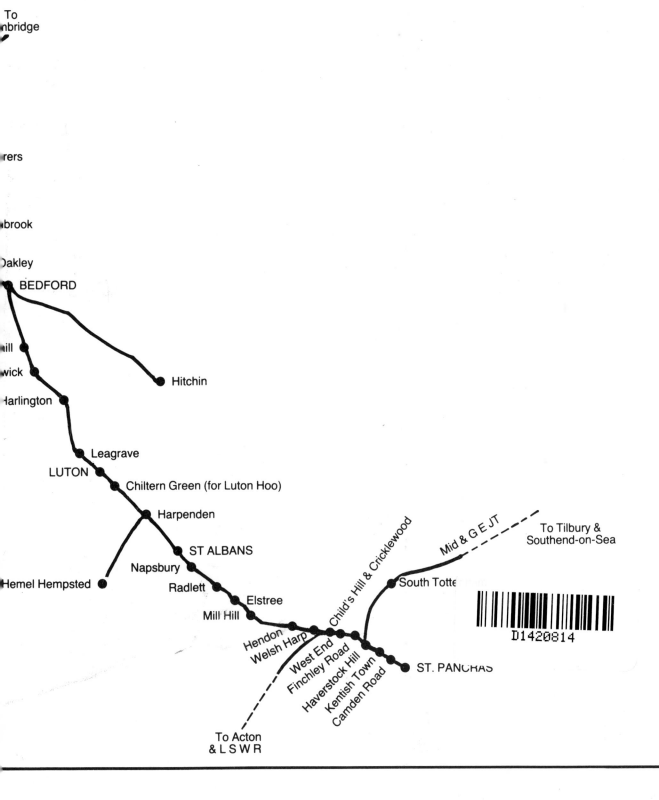

To nbridge

rers

brook

Oakley

BEDFORD

Hitchin

ill

wick

Harlington

Leagrave

LUTON

Chiltern Green (for Luton Hoo)

Harpenden

ST ALBANS

Child's Hill & Cricklewood

Mid & G E J T

To Tilbury &
Southend-on-Sea

Napsbury

South Totte

Hemel Hempsted

Radlett

Elstree

Mill Hill

Hendon

Welsh Harp

West End

Finchley Road

Haverstock Hill

Kentish Town

Camden Road

ST. PANCRAS

To Acton
& L S W R

MIDLAND LINE MEMORIES

BLOOMSBURY TRANSPORT HISTORY TITLES
General Editor Brian Jewell

The Metro-land trilogy by Dennis Edwards and Ron Pigram
Metro Memories
Romance of Metro-land
The Golden Years of the Metropolitan Railway

The Final Link (a pictorial history of the GW and GC Joint Line)
    by Dennis Edwards and Ron Pigram

Down the Line to Dover by Muriel V. Searle

London's Underground Suburbs by Dennis Edwards and Ron Pigram

A pictorial history of the Midland Railway
main line between London (St Pancras) and Derby

BRIAN RADFORD

BLOOMSBURY BOOKS
LONDON

To my daughter Elizabeth

Brian Radford comes from a railway family, and 'mis-spent' part of his youth in the pastime of train-spotting. He became very interested in the railway scene as a whole, and particularly in the historial aspects. He served an engineering apprenticeship at the Derby Locomotive Works before moving into the Locomotive Drawing Office of the CM&EE at Derby. There he was just in time to contribute, at a very junior level, to the last few years of work on the steam locomotives, mainly the BR Standard range, before the diesel locomotive took over the scene.

He is at present an assistant engineer in the design offices of the DM&EE at the Railway Technical Centre at Derby, where he has been involved in design work on both the High Speed Train and the Advanced Passenger Train.

His interests include music, opera singing and local history, but he devotes much of his spare time to the development of the Midland Railway Centre run by the Midland Railway Trust Ltd (a charitable trust) of which he is vice-chairman and acquisitions officer. The Trust is dedicated to the preservation of all things Midland by means of a working line, equipped as it would have been around the turn of the century, alongside a major museum complex on a 57-acre site.

Brian Radford hopes that the 'Midland Line Memories' encapsulated in this book merely in words and pictures may in some form become a reality again at the Midland Railway Centre.

This edition published 1988 by Bloomsbury Books an imprint of Godfrey Cave Associates Limited 42 Bloomsbury Street, London WC1B 3QJ under license from Baton Transport/ Cleveland Press

Printed in Yugoslavia

4

ACKNOWLEDGEMENTS
The author wishes to place on record his grateful thanks to all those friends, individuals and organizations who generously agreed to the loan of photographs and other material for use in this book. Special thanks go to Vic Forster, who kindly read through the manuscript and made many helpful suggestions, and also to Sue Grant for transforming my handwritten, and at times illegible, manuscript into the finished typescript.

The text is drawn from personal observations and a number of printed sources, principally the following: *Our Iron Roads* and *The Midland Railway – Its Rise and Progress* both by F. S. Williams; *Midland Railway Memories* by G. J. Pratt; *Derby Works and Midland Locomotives* by J. B. Radford; *Clinker's Register of Closed Passenger Stations and Goods Depots* and various official Midland Railway publications.

My very grateful thanks go to Sir John Betjeman, Kt, CBE, C Lit., and his publishers, John Murray Ltd, for permission to quote in full the poem 'Parliament Hill Fields' and my acknowledgements to Macmillan & Co. for the use of Thomas Hardy's poem 'The Levelled Churchyard' from his collected poems, edited by James Gibson.

Finally, my thanks to my wife and family for their forbearance over the period in which this book was being prepared.

Credits

The author gratefully acknowledges the following individuals and organizations who have willingly supplied illustrations for this book. Without their help the various subjects could not have been so well covered. The numbers quoted refer to page numbers, and the position on the page is indicated thus: T = Top, C = Centre, B = Bottom.

Author's collection: 7, 9, 12, 13, 15, 16, 19, 23, 24B, 26, 30, 32B, 34T, 34C, 36T, 38T, 41C, 41B, 42T, 42C, 43T, 43C, 45T right, 46C, 48T, 49B, 55B, 56T, 56C, 60T, 60C, 63T, 69T, 69C, 70C, 72T, 73T, 73C, 74T, 75T, 76T left & right, 80B, 83B right, 84C, 84B, 86B, 88C, 88B, 89T, 89B, 91, 92T, 93, 95T, 95B, 98C, 99T, 99C, 106C, 107C, 107B, 113T, 115B (courtesy D. Monk), 116T, 116C, 117T, 118, 119B, 120, 121B, 122C, 125T, 126T, 127T, 127C, 128T, 129, 134, 135B, 138C, 138B, 140, 141T left, 141B, 142C, 142B, 143B. V. R. Anderson: 52B, 65C, 65B, 66B, 67T, 79B, 80T, 83B left, 86C, 112C, 113C. S. Arnold: 33B. Bedfordshire County Record Office: 67C, 67B, 68T, 70T, 71B, 80C. Borough of Barnet Libraries: 43B, 45T left, 46T, 47T, 47B, 48C, 49T, 50B. Borough of Camden Libraries: 38B, 40C, 40B. W. Bradshaw (courtesy V. R. Webster): 107T, 108T. Breaston Libraries: 126B. British Rail (LMR): 21, 22, 24T, 25, 27, 35, 37B, 44, 51T, 54C, 72B, 82C, 83T, 104, 108B, 109, 112B, 123T, 125B. B. W. Brooksbank: 51B. R. J. Buckley: 121C, 128C. H. C. Casserley: 20, 29T, 31C, 32T, 36B, 45C, 59C, 61C, 62T, 62C, 66C, 68B, 81T, 82T, 85B, 87B, 89C, 105T, 106T, 124C. F. G. Cockman: 51C, 72C, 97B. Collectorcards: 56C. J. A. G. H. Coltas: 31B, 33C. W. Philip Conolly: 100B. Mrs J. V. Crisp: 123B, 126C. Derby Museums: 10, 29B,

32C, 39, 75B, 133B, 136C. Derbyshire Library Service: 141T right, 142T. T. J. Edgington: 47C. K. Fairey: 77, 86T, 87T. J. A. Fleming (Midland Railway Trust Archives): 46B, 87C, 137T, 137C. V. Forster: 28, 34B, 42B, 52T, 52C, 53T, 54T, 59T, 82B, 85T, 85C, 88T, 99B, 102C, 103T, 103C, 110T, 111C, 121T, 125C, 133T. W. L. Good: 122T. K. Grimes: 111T, 112T, 113B. L. Hanson (courtesy V. Forster): 84T. Harpenden Libraries: 59B, 60B. Hawker Siddeley/Brush E. E. Co.: 116B. J. F. Henton (courtesy V. Forster): 8, 123C, 124B. T. G. Hepburn (courtesy V. Forster): 135T, 135C. Home Counties Newspapers Ltd (courtesy S. Summerson): 62B, 63B. Kettering Libraries: 90T, 90B. Leicester Libraries & Museums: 96B, 101T, 102T, 110B, 111B, 114, 115T. M. L. Knighton Collection: 101B. London Brick Company Ltd: 69B, 70B. Loughborough Libraries: 117C, 117B. A. B. Longbottom: 131T. Luton Museums & Art Gallery: 64T. Market Harborough Library: 95C, 97T. Midland Railway Company Official (Author's Collection): 119T, 122B, 127B, 128B, 130, 131B(both), 131C, 132T, 132C, 136T, 136B. Midland Railway Trust Archives: 31T. National Monuments Records (Midland Railway Official): 55T, 71T, 105B. National Railway Museum (Midland Railway Official): 37T, 37C, 53B, 92B, 124T, 138T. H. B. Oliver: 48B, 63C. J. Osgood (courtesy V. R. Anderson): 68C. J. Palmer Collection: 137B. E. Pouteau: 33T. Rolls-Royce Ltd, Derby: 139B. S. Summerson: 17, 54B, 57, 58, 64B, 65T, 66T, 74B, 78, 79T, 81C, 81B. D. F. Tee Collection: 18, 38C, 40T, 41T, 45B, 50C, 61B, 75C, 79C, 98B. Valentine & Sons, Dundee: 73B, 132B, 139T. Vauxhall Motors Ltd, Luton: 64C. H. W. Webb: 94, 96T, 97C, 98T, 100T, 108C. V. R. Webster: 11, 14, 61T, 102B, 103B, 106B, 115C. W. W. Winter Ltd, Derby: 143T.

Contents

Parliament Hill Fields

Rumbling under blackened girders, Midland, bound for Cricklewood,
Puffed its sulphur to the sunset where that Land of Laundries stood.
Rumble under, thunder over, train and tram alternate go,
Shake the floor and smudge the ledger, Charrington, Sells, Dale and Co.,
Nuts and nuggets in the window, trucks along the lines below.

When the Bon Marché was shuttered, when the feet were hot and tired,
Outside Charrington's we waited, by the 'STOP HERE IF REQUIRED',
Launched aboard the shopping basket, sat precipitately down,
Rocked past Zwanziger the baker's, and the terrace blackish brown,
And the curious Anglo-Norman parish church of Kentish Town.

Till the tram went over thirty, sighting terminus again,
Past municipal lawn tennis and the bobble-hanging plane;
Soft the light suburban evening caught our ashlar-speckled spire,
Eighteen-sixty Early English, as the mighty elms retire
Either side of Brookfield Mansions flashing fine French-window fire.

Oh the after-tram-ride quiet, when we heard a mile beyond,
Silver music from the bandstand, barking dogs by Highgate Pond;
Up the hill where stucco houses in Virginia creeper drown –
And my childish wave of pity, seeing children carrying down
Sheaves of drooping dandelions to the courts of Kentish Town.

Sir John Betjeman
(from 'New Bats in Old Belfries')

1
The Midland Main Line to London

The Midland was a magnificent railway, standing head and shoulders above its rivals in many areas of activity. In the last quarter of the nineteenth century it ran the most comfortable trains, and catered for its travellers with the best of fare in superb dining cars. Meals fit for a king were cooked on board, with wines from its own vast cellars at Derby and St Pancras; while a cheaper repast was provided in the form of a luncheon basket for those of more modest means.

Its London terminus, St Pancras station, dwarfed the adjacent Great Northern's King's Cross terminus by its superb and lofty train shed and the magnificent Victorian Gothic Midland Grand Hotel building, the erection of which had heralded the end of an unhappy earlier period in the Midland's history when its trains ran into the capital only by courtesy of the Great Northern Railway.

The genesis of the Midland came about through the intuitive foresight of George Hudson, who was at one time fêted as the Railway King but later fell from grace; and indirectly through the influence of George Stephenson, the great engineer himself, who was at work behind the scenes.

Originally three small separate companies planned to embrace the then small market town of Derby with their individual schemes for railways. First in the field came the Midland Counties, promoted as something of a panic measure when the Notts and Derby coalmasters saw a new railway (the Leicester & Swannington) open up in Leicestershire between the

county town and Swannington to carry coals from places along its route quickly and more cheaply than the narrowboat canal-borne coal traffic from their coalfields. Although the line, when eventually opened, did not have the essential spur up the Erewash Valley to link in the largest coal-mines, it joined Derby and Nottingham on a route opened with due ceremony on 30 May 1839 amid great public interest.

The second section of the Midland Counties line ran from a junction near Long Eaton southwards via a magnificent new bridge over the river Trent, through the superb castellated portico of Red Hill Tunnel, some 133 yards long, and on to Loughborough and Leicester. It was completed at a later date and formally opened on 4 May 1840. A few days later, on 20 May, six trucks of coals from George Stephenson's collieries at Clay Cross arrived in Leicester, and the virtual monopoly of the Leicester & Swannington line was at an end.

The final portion of the Midland Counties line from Leicester to Rugby was viewed by the directors of the company on 18 May 1840 and opened without formal ceremony on 30 June that year. At Rugby the link to London & Birmingham Company's line was made to afford the first through route to the capital, with passenger trains from Leicester arriving in a bay platform, and goods traffic continuing on a parallel track to a direct connection a little further south.

However, a second company had by then started to operate a through service from Derby to London; this

Previous page
Midland style – Johnson 4-2-2 No. 688 at the head of an 'up' express in 1912.

Below
Platt's Crossing at Trent, showing the original alignment of the Midland Counties line of 1839.

Midland Counties Railway.

HOURS OF DEPARTURE.

AUGUST 1, 1842.

No. of Trains.	1	2	3	4	5	6	SUNDAYS 1	SUNDAYS 2	SUNDAYS 3	SUNDAYS 4
DOWN TRAINS.	1,2,3 class	1 & 2 class	1 & 2 class	1,2,3 class	1 & 2 class	1 & 2 class	1,2,3 class	1 & 2 class	1,2,3 class	1 & 2 class
DEPART FROM	am	am	am	am	pm	pm	am	am	pm	Mail pm
London.......	..	6 0	9 15	11 0	5 0	9 0	..	8 0	..	9 0
Birmingham..	..	8 30	..	1 15	6 0	..	..	..	..	..
Coventry.....	..	9 12	..	2 4	6 45	..	..	..	..	..
Rugby........	6 45	9 45	12 50	2 50	8 40	12 20	7 30	12 15	6 0	12 20
Ullesthorpe ...	7 5	10 0	1 10	3 10	9 0	12 40	7 50	12 35	6 20	12 40
Broughton...	7 15	10 8	..	3 18	..	..	8 0	..	6 30	..
Wigston	7 25	10 20	..	3 30	..	..	8 12	..	6 42	..
Leicester	7 45	10 40	1 45	3 50	9 30	1 10	8 30	1 10	7 0	1 10
Syston	7 58	10 50	2 0	4 5	9 40	1 25	8 45	1 25	7 15	1 25
Sileby	8 6	11 0	..	4 15	..	..	8 54	..	7 24	..
Barrow.......	8 13	11 5	..	4 25	..	..	9 2	..	7 32	..
Loughboro'...	8 20	11 15	2 18	4 35	10 0	1 45	9 10	1 45	7 40	1 45
Kegworth.....	8 32	11 25	2 30	4 50	10 12	..	9 22	2 0	7 52	..
ARRIVE AT										
Nottingham...	9 15	12 10	3 15	5 30	10 50	4 10	10 0	2 30	8 30	4 10
Derby	9 0	12 10	3 15	5 30	10 50	2 49	10 0	2 30	8 30	2 49
Sheffield	11 45	2 45	5 30	8 15	..	5 0	..	5 30	..	5 0
Leeds	1 15	4 0	7 0	9 45	..	6 19	..	7 15	..	6 19
York.........	2 0	4 45	7 45	..	..	6 40	..	7 30	..	6 40
Darlington...	5 15	7 0	..	..	..	9 25	..	..	..	9 20
Hull.........	3 45	6 45	9 0	..	..	8 36	..	8 50	..	8 36
Manchester ...	5 0	6 20	8 45	..	..	8 40	..	9 30	..	..

No. of Trains.	1	2	3	4	5	6	SUNDAYS 1	SUNDAYS 2	SUNDAYS 3	SUNDAYS 4
UP TRAINS.	1,2,3 class	1 & 2 class	1,2,3 class	1 & 2 class	1 & 2 class	1,2,3 class	1 & 2 class	1,2,3 class	1 & 2 class
DEPART FROM	am	am	am	am	pm	Mail pm	am	am	pm	Mail pm
Manchester ...	..	..	7 0	10 0	..	4 45	..	..	..	..
Hull..........	..	..	6 15	10 40	..	4 55	..	..	..	5 0
Darlington....	..	..	6 15	9 15	..	3 30	..	..	..	3 30
York.........	..	..	8 45	12 0	..	6 19	..	6 45	..	6 19
Leeds	..	6 0	9 30	1 0	..	7 9	..	7 30	..	7 9
Sheffield	..	7 30	10 45	1 50	..	8 12	..	8 45	..	8 12
Derby	8 15	10 30	1 15	4 40	7 30	10 40	6 45	12 15	7 0	10 40
Nottingham...	8 15	10 30	1 15	4 40	7 30	9 0	6 45	12 15	7 0	9 0
Kegworth.....	8 50	11 0	1 48	5 13	8 5	..	7 25	12 45	7 35	..
Loughboro'...	9 2	11 10	2 0	5 25	8 17	11 20	7 39	1 0	7 47	11 20
Barrow.......	9 13	..	..	..	8 28	..	7 49	..	7 58	..
Sileby	9 20	11 20	..	..	8 35	..	7 55	..	8 5	..
Syston	9 30	11 30	2 20	5 45	8 45	11 45	8 5	1 20	8 15	11 45
Leicester......	9 50	11 50	2 40	6 0	9 0	12 0	8 30	1 40	8 30	12 0
Wigston	10 0	..	..	..	9 10	..	8 40	..	8 40	..
Broughton....	10 15	..	..	..	9 25	..	8 58	..	8 55	..
Ullesthorpe ...	10 30	12 15	3 15	6 30	9 40	12 30	9 10	2 10	9 10	12 30
ARRIVE AT										
Rugby	11 0	12 50	3 40	7 0	10 0	12 50	9 30	2 30	9 30	12 50
Coventry	12 35	1 34	6 26	9 2	12 27	..	..	..	..	..
Birmingham ..	1 45	2 30	7 45	10 15	1 30	..	..	..	..	..
London	3 15	6 0	7 45	11 15	..	5 0	1 30	7 30	..	5 0

SUNDAYS.

NOTTINGHAM TO DERBY.	1,2,3 class	1 & 2 class	1 & 2 class	1,2,3 class	1 & 2 class	1,2,3 class	1,2,3 class	1 & 2 class
DEPART FROM	am	am	pm	pm	pm	am	pm	pm
Nottingham	7 20	10 40	2 45	6 0	9 0	9 0	7 0	9 0
Beeston	7 29	10 49	2 54	6 9	9 9	9 9	7 9	9 9
Long-Eaton	7 38	10 58	3 3	6 18	..	9 18	7 18	..
Sawley	7 46	11 5	3 11	6 26	9 23	9 26	7 26	9 23
Borrowash	7 55	11 15	3 20	6 35	..	9 35	7 35	..
Spondon	..	11 20	..	6 40	..	9 40	7 40	..
ARRIVE AT								
Derby	8 5	11 25	3 30	6 45	9 40	9 45	7 45	9 40

DERBY TO NOTTINGHAM.	1 & 2 class	1,2,3 class	1 & 2 class	1,2,3 class	1 & 2 class	1,2,3 class	1 & 2 class	1,2,3 class
DEPART FROM	am	am	p.m.	p m	p m	a m	a m	pm
Derby	3 30	9 0	1 30	4 50	7 40	3 30	9 15	8 0
Spondon	..	9 5	1 35	4 55	..	..	9 20	8 5
Borrowash	..	9 11	1 41	5 3	7 53	..	9 26	8 11
Sawley	..	9 20	1 50	5 10	8 0	..	9 35	8 20
Long-Eaton	..	9 28	1 58	5 20	8 10	..	9 43	8 28
Beeston	..	9 37	2 7	5 28	8 18	..	9 52	8 37
ARRIVE AT								
Nottingham	4 10	9 45	2 15	5 35	8 25	4 10	10 0	8 45

*** Third Class Carriages will be attached at Leicester to the Down Train No. 1, and detached at that place from the Down Train No. 2. Also, be detached at Leicester from the Up Train No. 1, excepting on Saturdays, when they will be attached at Leicester to the Up Train No. 4, calling at all the intermediate Stations except Wigston.

[J. BURTON, PRINTER, HAYMARKET, LEICESTER.]

BY ORDER, J. F. BELL, Secretary.

was the Birmingham & Derby Junction Railway whose tracks linked in with the London & Birmingham line at Hampton Junction. The line was opened to the public on 12 August 1839 and competition between the two companies for London traffic became so ruinous that both MCR and B & DJR finances were seriously strained.

The third company (with plans to link Derby with Leeds) was the North Midland, which opened the first section of line between Derby and Rotherham on 11 May 1840; the final section to Leeds was opened for passenger traffic on Wednesday, 1 July 1840.

These three companies eventually came together to form the Midland Railway Company on 10 May 1844. However, the Midland slumped to near-bankruptcy after a great upheaval, initially caused by George Stephenson's death at Chesterfield on 12 August 1848, and continued by George Hudson's resignation the following year over allegations that

various company accounts had been 'manipulated'.

The new chairman, John Ellis, brought a gradual change of fortunes, and by 1851 a wave of optimism was being experienced in railway circles. The scheme for building a Leicester to Hitchin line was revived; this had replaced an earlier South Midland Railway scheme by the Midland and local interests to link Leicester with the London & Birmingham line between Roade and Blisworth. Originally raised by an 1847 Act but relinquished in July 1850, it was resuscitated by the Leicester and Bedford party, a prominent member of which was Mr William Whitbread, who owned one-eighth of all the land necessary for the building. With the threat that failure to take up the proposal again would lead to a rival company taking control, and the imperative need of the Midland to secure an improved outlet to London for its constantly growing freight traffic, the Midland sought an amalgamation with the London & North Western Company in a bill introduced to Parliament in 1853. However, a Select Committee advised the House against the formation of very large companies, despite the fact that the Midland had to utilize its connecting facilities at Rugby to forward both freight and passenger traffic to London; the latter comprised only eight weekday and four Sunday trains in each direction.

Thus the Midland's Leicester & Hitchin Extension Committee bent to the task and the Leicester & Hitchin Bill had a relatively easy passage through both Houses and received Royal Assent on 4 August 1853. The new line was authorized from a junction with the existing Midland main line near Wigston to a junction with the Great Northern Company's line at Hitchin. At Bedford the LNWR branch from Bletchley was to be crossed on the level; the river Nene in Northamptonshire was to be spanned by a viaduct with a clear span of 350 feet, and a bridge across the river Ise was to have a span of 90 feet.

Only two contracts were involved in the whole length of line, one for the

880-yard-long Warden Tunnel, let to John Knowles of Sheffield, while the most famous of railway contractors, Thomas Brassey, received the contracts for all the remaining works. Construction began in April 1854 on Whitbread land in the parishes of Cardington and Warden, Bedfordshire, and the lack of a public house (an essential feature indeed) in the area was remedied by the conversion of a house in a tiny hamlet called Ireland, some two miles south of Warden Tunnel; the hostelry still stands today.

In the summer of 1854 many labourers left for more remunerative employment in the harvest fields. This migration was followed by a very wet autumn, and agreement was reached to reduce the depth of major cuttings to conserve labour and finance, resulting in more undulation on the route than was originally planned. Kibworth, Desborough and Sharnbrook, with its long climb of 1 in 119 from the south, proved the most formidable of obstacles, while the rivers and valley had to be spanned by substantial viaducts, with some foundation works shifting during construction. The

Below
'A motley crew'. Midland permanent-way gang at Nottingham about 1899 with the responsibility for keeping in good order the tracks laid by the navvies.

Above
South Wigston station – typical of the
Midland Counties line stations on the
section between Leicester and Rugby.

Great Ouse had to be crossed no
fewer than six times before Bedford
was reached, where a right-angle level
crossing with the London & North
Western Railway was engineered on
its line from Bletchley.

Inevitably there were a number of
accidents during the construction
works, and at various times 'irregular
and riotous conduct of the labourers in
the railway workings', which resulted
in the swearing-in of special constables
in various parishes. Drunkenness,
poaching and petty thieving were
common among the navvies; one of
them was charged with stealing a
sleeper worth 9d (about 4p), for which
he received fourteen days' hard labour
as a first offender.

Frederick S. Williams, in his
Victorian masterpiece of railway
literature *Our Iron Roads*, penned a
portrait of the old-time navvy from
personal observation:

The word 'navvie' is an abridgement of
'navigator', a class of men first employed
in the construction of the canals that
immediately preceded the railway era.
Many were 'bankers' from the lowlands
of Lincolnshire and Cambridgeshire,
where they had made the banks and cut
the canals by which waste lands were
recovered from marsh and sea. The
wages offered by railway contractors
drew great numbers of other men from
all parts of the country, especially from
the hills of Lancashire and Yorkshire,

and they had the boldest characteristics
of the Anglo-Saxon stock. Their great
strength, their knowledge of embanking,
boring and well sinking, and their
familiarity with the nature of clays and
rocks, gave them special qualifications
for making railway earthworks.

The navvie of the period wandered
from one place to another. He usually
wore a white felt hat with the brim
turned up, a velveteen or jean square-
tailed coat, a scarlet plush waistcoat with
little black spots, and a bright-coloured
kerchief round his herculean neck when,
as often happened, it was not left
entirely bare. His corduroy breeches
were retained in position by a leathern
strap round the waist, and were tied and
buttoned at the knee, displaying beneath
a solid calf and foot encased in strong
high-laced boots. Joining together in a
'butty gang' some ten or twelve of these
men would take a contract to cut out and
remove so much 'dirt' – as they
denominated earth-cutting – fixing their
price according to the character of the
'stuff', and the distance to which it had
to be wheeled and tipped. The contract
taken, every man put himself to his
mettle: if any were found skulking, or
not putting forth his full working power,
he was ejected from the 'gang'. Their
powers of endurance and their
consumption of flesh food were alike
enormous. They seemed to disregard
danger, and they were as reckless of
their earnings as of their lives. Pay day
was usually once a fortnight, when a
large amount of their earnings was

11

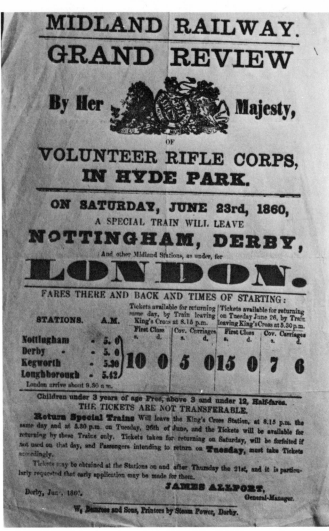

Above left
Interesting early excursion leaflet for the original Midland route into London (Euston) via Rugby. Note the early starting time of 5.15 a.m.!

Above right
A second leaflet from the early period, this time via Hitchin and the Great Northern to King's Cross, with an even earlier starting time.

squandered in dissipation. A sum equal to £1000 a mile on all the railways of England, has, it is said, thus been wasted. Ignorant and violent as some of them were, they were open-handed to their comrades, and would share their last penny with their friends who were in distress. They also often had a shrewdness, and even a cunning, which got many a one into a scrape and many another out.

The extension was eventually opened on Wednesday, 15 April 1857 for mineral traffic, with goods traffic starting a week later. Passenger services commenced on Thursday, 7 May with due ceremony; the first train of eighteen carriages left the Great Northern Station at Hitchin at 7.33 a.m. carrying a red flag. It arrived in Bedford St John's (LNW) at 8.15 a.m. and at Leicester at 10.50 a.m. A second train comprising sixteen first class and fourteen second class carriages left Bedford for Leicester at the more sober hour of 9.02 a.m. The Bedford Militia enlivened proceedings as they played martial airs and other music from an open carriage behind the locomotive, while the mayor of Bedford rode in a beautiful coach in

the rest of the train. Since the mayor had directed that all shops be locked and shuttered for the day and businesses closed, there were plenty of people on hand to view the proceedings.

No public announcement of the event appears to have been made at Leicester and the first information that the local people had of it was when crowds of jubilant visitors invaded the streets in the middle of the day; for apart from the two specials from Bedford, another had come from Kettering and Market Harborough and a fourth from Hitchin. For many of the passengers it was their first railway journey and they were experiencing a novelty that Leicester people had had over twenty-five years before!

While Bedford dignitaries were entertained to lunch at the station, ordinary passengers thronged the streets and hotels and eating-houses were vigorously invaded. Nearly 5000 seats were sold for the opening and six locomotives and more than a hundred carriages were used. Bedford made a thoughtful gesture by ensuring that the children from the local workhouse participated in the event, and had a good look round Leicester and a meal in the Temperance Hall afterwards. Regular services commenced the following day.

This honeymoon period however soon turned sour, for the Midland discovered that their trains were to be treated in a cavalier fashion, Great Northern goods and mineral traffic almost always being given precedence over the Midland's own trains going through to the relatively new terminus at King's Cross; although for a number of years the Midland through passenger service continued to go via Rugby, to the LNWR station at Euston rather than via the new route, where the Midland's passengers were forced to change trains, for there were neither through trains nor through booking of tickets. The Midland chairman pressed for running powers for his own trains into King's Cross, and

eventually the heads of an agreement were signed on 2 December 1857 and through trains began running on Monday, 1 February 1858.

Midland traffic expanded to such an extent that the company began to search for a suitable site near King's Cross on which to build a separate goods station, and found it at Agar Town in St Pancras parish; a triangular piece of semi-waste ground some three-quarters of a mile north-west of King's Cross, bounded by the North London Railway, the Great Northern Railway and the Regent's Canal.

In February 1859 a special Agar Town Committee came into existence and a 27-acre site was bought; this, together with a further purchase, enabled the construction of the orginal Midland goods station to commence, subject to the necessary parliamentary approval. Thus a major step forward was the passing of the Act on 25 May

Left
A signed portrait of James Allport, Midland chairman from 1853 to 1857 and again from 1860 to 1880.

1860 enabling the Midland to construct 'a station in the Parish of St Pancras, London and to effect arrangements with the Great Northern and North London Railways and the Regent's Canal to facilitate its construction and use'. New capital of £200,000 was authorized in shares and £66,000 on loan.

On 20 June 1862 Seymour Clarke, general manager of the Great Northern Railway, wrote to James Allport (his opposite number on the Midland) stating that he had visited the new goods station, observed its approaching completion and had seen rail access from the GNR installed. He therefore called on the Midland to vacate his premises forthwith. By 1 July Allport was able to report to his traffic committee that coal traffic could be removed to the new Midland depot immediately. However, the GN was already harassing Midland pasengers; in two instances passengers had to board trains from the ballast level at King's Cross. After complaints, this was rectified merely by the erection of a platform two planks wide. Coupled with this came the long delays accorded to Midland trains, in particular to the

excursion traffic which had grown apace in the intervening years. Queues formed on the new GN four-track section north of Holloway, while Midland passengers had to sit and watch GN trains take precedence in entering the King's Cross terminus.

The Midland were goaded into fresh efforts to find a solution and, despite the consideration of a quadrupling of the GN main line towards which Midland was asked to pay £60,000 per annum (a £40,000 increase on the then current figure), a decision was taken that the most economical long-term solution would be the construction of a completely independent extension of the Midland line from Bedford southwards to a brand-new London terminus. On 14 October 1862 the Midland Board took a far-sighted and courageous step and set the plan in motion.

Despite the sad death of the Midland chairman less than two weeks later, the plan was pressed forward and the Midland Railway (Extension to London) Bill was presented to the Commons Select Committee on 3 March 1863. No less than seventeen petitions were raised against it by

Below
Bedford, as it was on 20 April 1935, showing the alignment of the original platforms which gave access to the Hitchin line.

various bodies – railway, canal, church and local authorities – but the Midland evidence in support of the proposals was soundly based and Allport himself gave evidence in the House of Lords. Eventually the case for the Bill was found proven and Royal Assent was given on 22 June 1863. The capital raised for the line amounted to £1,750,000 in shares and £583,330 on loan.

On 14 July the Midland's engineers and solicitors were instructed to take all steps necessary to obtain sufficient land for four lines of railway between the south end of Hampstead Tunnel and the goods station in St Pancras and negotiations were put in hand for the rest of the route. Eight contracts were let by tender for the construction plus a further contract for the 716-yard Ampthill Tunnel, let to John Knowles of Sheffield. Messrs Brassey & Ballard were contracted to build the section from Bedford to within 14 miles 40 chains of London, the other sections further south going to Messrs Waring

Brothers and J. Firbank, while A. W. Ritson was given the last section of 1 mile 70 chains right into St Pancras goods station yard, 60 chains north of Euston Road.

The first sod was turned on Harrisons Estate to the west of Kentish Town Road and almost overnight the area was covered with huts, workshops and offices, while a brickworks was established to turn the clay hacked from the earthworks into bricks for the construction.

In advance of completion of the new lines work went ahead to complete the new facilities at St Pancras for goods and merchandise traffic; these were brought into use on 2 January 1865 to replace those provided by the GNR at King's Cross.

William Henry Barlow, the Midland Company's resident engineer, reported that although at that one location 400 men and 27 horses were hard at work, progress was too slow. The contractor's works manager was replaced, more men and animals were employed, and

there was an undoubted improvement.

At the southern end Ritson struggled with his contract, but was eventually beaten by rising costs and inadequate capital reserves and the contract was re-let to John Ashwell on 11 April 1866.

Belsize Tunnel, 1 mile and 66 yards long, was a major engineering feat, involving the sinking of five shafts (reputedly done by miners from County Durham) to be followed by the actual tunnelling work which began in April 1865. These operations were not completed without great difficulty; some of the navvies worked for two days and a night at a stretch – a tribute to their incredible fitness and stamina. The last brick was laid by Allport on a tour of the new lines on 27 June 1867.

Work on the other contracts fell behind schedule, mainly because of bad weather, shortage of bricks and difficulties in securing land by purchase. Waring Brothers eventually fell foul of a combination of circumstances (as had Ritson at the southern end) which resulted in their relinquishing their contract, which Joseph Firbank promptly took up.

Brassey & Ballard completed the two tracks throughout from Bedford to 14½ miles from London on 24 August 1867 although the construction of the intermediate stations, goods depots and other facilities was well behind schedule. The tracks for the whole Extension were completed by the end of August and were formally opened on Saturday, 7 September 1867 when, at 10 a.m., a special double-headed train set out from Bedford. On board were Midland officials, representatives of the contractors and a number of drivers and guards, and the train drew into St Pancras goods station to a resounding cheer from the assembled workmen.

Regular traffic began on the night of Monday, 9 September and consisted of about a dozen main-line trains diverted at Bedford Junction from the old route to Hitchin. Little traffic was allowed during the day because of the vast amount of unfinished work and finishing off by the contractors' work forces and the completion of stations. Still to come was the final 60-chain St Pancras Extension and the erection of the grand passenger terminus fronting Euston Road, which will be described in the next chapter.

Local passenger traffic between Bedford and Moorgate Street began regular working from 13 July 1868. All

trains called at Kentish Town, where
the locomotives were uncoupled and
the trains taken forward by the
Midland's new condensing 4-4-0 tank
locomotives (of a type built by Messrs
Beyer Peacock of Manchester and
supplied also to the Metropolitan
Railway) via St Paul's Road Junction,
King's Cross Junction and thence via
the Metropolitan Railway to Moorgate
Street.

Riding on the engine on the first
public train to use the route was
Frederick S. Williams, author of *The
Midland Railway – Its Rise and
Progress* and *Our Iron Roads*, both of
which went through many editions in
their day. His description of the
journey is a peerless piece of Victorian
prose and is here reproduced in its
entirety as a fitting conclusion to our
opening chapter:

A railway being completed and about to
be devoted to public use, is opened.
How this is sometimes done we are able
to tell from our own experience.

'All right, sir,' said the engine-driver,
as his eye rested on a brief official order
we had handed to him, and which bore a
signature which has talismanic powers
with all Midland Railway people. 'All
right, sir; we shall be off directly.' The
train, spic and span new – the lot worth
perhaps £5000 – was standing one
Monday morning on the new rails by the
new platform, under the new glass and
iron shed of the recently enlarged station
at Bedford, and was about to take its
first run to London; in fact, to open the
line for passenger traffic. Being afflicted
with what Mr Cobden would have called
'a craze' for railways, we had been
seized with a passion somewhat akin to
that which animated the breasts of those
little boys who, on the opening of the
new Westminster Bridge, ran a neck-and-
neck race that they might achieve the
distinction of being the first to cross, and
we had resolved to be the first of that
great army of the British public who
would pass and repass upon this new
railway between the Midlands and the
metropolis. The authorities, with we
suppose an amiable consideration for

Above
Luton station on 28 June 1961 as Stanier
class five 45238 hauls a 'down' fitted freight
past the old goods station which opened
for business on 16 December 1867, before
the passenger traffic commenced.

the eccentricities of literary men, gave the requisite consent; and so we mounted the engine with a sense of satisfaction that by our very position on the train we should be the first unofficials by the first train that ever went by the new route from Bedford to London.

The Superintendent of the company, Mr Needham, and Mr Vaughan, from the locomotive department, had joined us. The time was up. The driver's hand was on the lever, and the usual signal to start had just been given, when the stout lady – the inevitable stout lady who generally appears on railway platforms at the last moment – hove in sight. The fireman growled, the guard shouted, we were all delayed; but eventually, perhaps somewhat hurriedly, the lady was stowed away somewhere – nobody cared where – and the train was off.

We crossed the sluggish Ouse near the great engineering establishment of Messrs Howard; went by a bridge over the London and North Western line from Bletchley to Bedford; saw on our left the historic village of Elstow, the birthplace of the 'immortal tinker'; and were soon on the long straight bank that leads to Ampthill tunnel and station. At Ampthill all the little world of curiosity or of idleness has gathered to be spectators of our triumph. The driver looks at his watch; the fireman at the time-table; and it is announced that though we left Bedford two minutes late (it was the stout lady who detained us),

we are now in time. 'Ah,' says the driver with a knowing smile, 'I'd sooner pick up one minute than drop two.' The passengers are in; Mr Needham reports progress; and again we start. Soon we are running on the summit of another long establishment, from which we can see the line far before us, and the country far around us. Occasionally a group of platelayers part to the right and left for us to pass; the village girls pause upon the country road, and shade their bright faces from the sun as they gaze upon the first train that has ever run that way; the old farmer rests his arms upon the top of his homestead gate, and thinks perhaps how things have changed since he 'wur a boy'; the larks fly off with long and quivering wing; and now and then a partridge rises and whirrs away. A short cutting and we are at the pretty village of Harlington. 'Very good time,' remarks our friend of the loco. department; 'three minutes to spare.'

We have scarcely left Harlington when right and left we see the long line of breezy chalk hills which tell us we are approaching 'the backbone of England'. The Great Northern crosses it at Hitchen, the North Western at Tring; but there is a dip in the range before us, and we seem, as we run round a hill artificially scarped and terraced, called Wanlud's Bank, as if we should slip between them. But though the engineers have doubtless done their best, they have had to make two deep cuttings in

Below
A Kirtley 2-4-0 No. 15, dating back to April 1868 heads an 'up' express through Radlett station in about 1920.

the chalk, a lesser and a larger, to let us through; and at the southern end of the latter we see the signals and buildings of Leagrave. We now cross the ancient Icknield Way, which Roman soldiers built, and which Roman feet have trodden. We see on the right the Great Northern branch from Dunstable and Luton to Hatfield, and in a few minutes we descry the suburban villas that climb the hills that rise around the thriving town of Luton. Here a large number of people have come to bid us welcome, and to hail our departure.

We are just starting, when someone rushes up to the engine-driver and exclaims: 'There goes the Great Northern train, and they say they'll be in London first.' We looked, and certainly the Great Northern train was in full cry. Our driver smiled as he turned on the steam, evidently not much affected by the challenge; but our less responsible stoker pulls backs the fiery jaws of the furnace, and on to the seething sea of flame he flings fresh coals with un-

dissembled satisfaction. Not far from us for a considerable distance runs the single line of the Great Northern branch; there we could observe its train hotly pursuing its onward course, and then we lost sight of it, and at length reached St Albans.

We are descending a long incline of 1 in 176; and, though the steam is only half on, the lever is sometimes at 'SHUT', we go faster than before. At Radlett we pause, partly to take in water – 'Just a sup,' says the driver, 'to make sure,' though there is plenty in the tender; we meet the first down passenger train, and then Elstree station is before us. We enter Elstree tunnel, 1060 yards in length, and soon after are under the green glass roof of the Mill Hill station. Here the fireman whiles away the momentary delay by opening wide the furnace door, inserting therein a long iron hoe, and raking to and fro the seething mass of white-hot coals and red eddying flames. He then moistens his arid clay from a tin can which he has

Above
A fine study of Johnson 'spinner', 4-2-2 No. 27 at the head of a rather mixed train of stock which includes a Pullman car, as it enters Child's Hill & Cricklewood station in about 1895.

kept warm upon a little shelf near the
fire – a vessel to which he and the driver
have frequently repaired during the
journey up, and the ownership of which
seems to be held in a sort of joint stock
coffee company (limited).

Fifteen minutes more, and we are in
Belsize tunnel, and overhead spreads
the ancient demesne of Belsize.
Haverstock Hill and Kentish Town
stations come next, and at last we pause
for a moment to change our engine for
one that consumes most of its own
smoke and steam, and is intended for
special use on the Metropolitan. At
Moorgate Street we say good-bye to our
companions in travel. 'If the historian of
the future' we tell them, 'asks you who
opened the London and Bedford
Railway, mind you tell them the truth. It
was not you, gentlemen, you are only
the officers of the Midland Company.
We represent the great British public.
We pay for everything. There are lots of
the great British public in those carriages
behind; but we are first, and we opened
the line from Bedford to London.' And
so, with cheery words, we parted.

2
St Pancras – Railway Gothic

The St Pancras Extension proved to be a complex, difficult and rather expensive part of the move to bring the Midland line right into the heart of London and provide a fitting terminus which still today effectively dwarfs the adjacent King's Cross station of the Great Northern in typically grand Midland fashion, and perhaps expresses the exhilaration of being eventually freed from the frustrating experiences of former years at the hands of this rival company.

W. H. Barlow, the Midland Company's resident engineer, was confronted with a number of major

Previous page
Midland Gothic – the Midland Grand Hotel, with the Station to the right, as it was in about 1885.

Below
The massive train shed under construction by the Butterley Company in 1866, showing the movable wooden staging used in the erection of the main roof-arch members.

engineering problems. To reach the passenger station site in the eastern part of Somers Town, the line would need to be extended through rubbish heaps and the slums and sordid tenements of Agar Town, obliquely across the Regent's Canal, over the old St Pancras burial ground and then over the river Fleet which bounded the old St Pancras Road. The canal dictated either a high-level station some 20 feet above Euston Road or a low-level one some 20 feet below. Since the latter would have required very expensive tunnelling beneath the canal and surrounding area, Barlow chose the former solution and negotiations and discussions began with various authorities; not least of these was Vestry of St Pancras who negotiated a £15,000 bond from the Midland against damage to the local sewers. There was much public resistance to the disturbance of remains in the closed burial ground of St Pancras Chapel, and the

Metropolitan Railway's engineer, John Fowler, strongly attacked the proposals for the Midland's connecting line and the junction at King's Cross (Met). However, the Midland Board persisted in its efforts to overcome the problems and by the end of 1865 matters were very much more promising.

The contract for the Extension was placed with Waring Brothers on 12 February 1866, the price being just over £319,000. A special clause provided for timber staging to be erected across the burial ground; no part of it was to touch any grave, and no grave was to be disturbed without an order in writing from Barlow, subject to agreement with the appropriate authorities. During the period March to June 1866 the dreadful slum properties at Agar Town and Somers Town were cleared away and also, despite the assurances given, some graves in St Pancras burial ground were disturbed, so that when

work started skulls and bones were
seen lying about and a passer-by saw
an open coffin inside which gleamed a
bright tress of hair. A great scandal
was caused and the Midland had to
arrange for a hasty reburial. The
architect in charge was A. W.
Blomfield, who sent one of his young
assistants to see that all was reverently
done. That assistant was Thomas
Hardy, later the famous novelist and
poet, who was to write two poems
recalling the event, 'In the Cemetery'
and the one quoted below, 'The
Levelled Churchyard'.

*O Passenger, pray list and catch
 Our sighs and piteous groans,
Half stifled in this jumbled patch
 Of wrenched memorial stones!*

*We late-lamented, resting here,
 Are mixed to human jam,
And each to each exclaims in fear,
 'I know not which I am!'*

*The wicked people have annexed
 The verses on the good;
A roaring drunkard sports the text
 Teetotal Tommy should!*

*Where we are huddled none can trace,
 And if our names remain,
They pave some path or porch or place
 Where we have never lain!*

*Here's not a modest maiden elf
 But dreads the final Trumpet,
Lest half of her should rise herself,
 And half some sturdy strumpet!*

*From restorations of Thy fane,
 From smoothings of Thy sward,
From zealous Churchmen's pick and plane
 Deliver us O Lord! Amen!*

The tunnelling of one line down to
meet the then steam-tractioned
Metropolitan Railway (today now
part of the Inner Circle) continued
according to plan, while the
construction of some 16,000 square
yards of brick arching carrying the
tracks past St Pancras gasworks and
over the old St Pancras road also
proceeded.

Meanwhile, the thousands of
working-class people displaced by the
clearance work were herded together
in much overcrowded conditions in
nearby districts; there was a cholera
outbreak because of the foulness of
the river Fleet, which was later
contained in a cast-iron sewer
beneath the new station.

As to the station itself, once the
Midland's engineer, William Henry
Barlow (1812–1902), had established
that the high-level station was to be
the design, used his imagination to
the full and produced what remained

the largest single-span station roof in
the world for nearly a century. The
most interesting architectural feature
is its two-storey layout, for the
working station area hides below it a
second level comprising an enormous
cellar, and since much of the Midland
traffic in those days consisted of beer
for the inhabitants of the metropolis
from Burton-upon-Trent in
Staffordshire, the supporting columns
for the station level above were
placed at a distance dictated by the
standard beer barrel of the day.

The construction of the station
itself required some 60 million bricks,
9000 tons of steel and iron and
fourteen different kinds of stone. The
single-span roof, a clear 240 feet
wide, has an apex height of 100 feet.
To erect it the workmen, under
Barlow's direction, utilized a colossal
wooden scaffolding running on rails;
this was made from 1000 tons of
timber and 80 tons of iron ties, and
carried cranes and lifting jacks. As
each set of arches was erected, the
whole erection was moved forward
an inch at a time by men armed with
crowbars.

The great cast-iron arched ribs and
supporting ties which form the vast
roof, covering an area of 165,000
square feet, were made by the
Butterley Company at their ironworks
in Derbyshire, and today it stands,
after recent repainting and renovation,
as a tribute to the craftsmanship and
art of those ironfounders of the last
century.

After erection, the scaffolding was
taken down, but it remains there in
the form of paving blocks beneath
the carriageway surface leading up to
the station. One hundred steam
cranes, 6000 men and 1000 horses
laboured for four years to produce
the impressive end result that is St
Pancras station.

When Barlow designed the train
shed he also made provision for a
magnificent hotel to stand at its
southern end fronting onto Euston
Road. In 1863 the Midland Company
had held a competition for the
design; George (later Sir) Gilbert
Scott was the winner, despite the fact
that he ignored the conditions and

MANUFACTURED BY THE BUTTERLEY COMPANY

1867

DERBYSHIRE

presented plans for an hotel twice the specified size. No doubt the Midland Board was impressed by the grandeur of the whole scheme and saw it as a fitting crown to the glory of what was to be at last their very own London terminus.

Work on the hotel began in 1868, but was held up at various stages because of difficulties with the supply of materials. The building was opened to the public for the first time on 5 May 1873 as the Midland Grand Hotel, although the west wing was to take another three years to complete. It was easily the best hotel at the time in the whole of London, with its pinnacles and ornate spires pointing heavenwards, pointed arch windows, castellated fringes, decorative pillars and steeply pitched roofs surmounted by scores of elaborate chimneys, looking for all the world like a railway cathedral.

Inside, its 400 bedrooms had the finest in elegant furnishings by Gillow. It had beautiful high vaulted ceilings, intertwining double staircase,

carved oak doors, marble-lined walls, paintings and sculptures, gaslit chandeliers and miles of deep pile carpeting. Modern features, such as electric bells and hydraulic lifts (quaintly called 'ascending rooms') abounded. There was the best Elkington plate, Royal Worcester porcelain and furniture supplied by Gillow; no less than ten pianos for the best sitting rooms supplied by Erards, and richly coloured decorations by Mr Sang – which some of the press condemned as 'too loud'. The *Railway News*, announcing the hotel and the appointment of a *maître d'hotel*, reported that 'the apartments are magnificent and the charges moderate'. At first the charge for a room, breakfast, dinner and attendance was 14s (70p), while a table d'hote dinner at 5s (25p) was selected for special mention. Ordinary bed and breakfast was 5s per night, a four-course lunch 3s 6d and a six course, haute cuisine dinner with wine a mere 5s 6d.

Above
Superb photograph of the early stages of construction of the Midland Grand Hotel, showing an absorbing row of advertisement hoardings.

Above
The completed train shed before
opening, showing early slotted post
signals. As yet there is no sign of the hotel
at the far end.

The station itself opened for
business on 1 October 1868 (although
much of the building work was still to
be completed) and the first train was
the night mail from Leeds which
arrived without fuss or ceremony at
4.15 a.m. on that historic day, marked
by the merest mention in the press;
the *London Illustrated News* simply
informed its readers that the station
was 'the largest in the world'.
Overnight the whole of the Midland
staff, together with tickets, furniture,
carriages and other property, were
transferred from King's Cross to these
new and impressive premises.

The first 'new' train to leave St
Pancras was the 10 a.m. express for
Manchester, calling at Kentish Town
(as almost all expresses then did) to
provide connections from outer
London and the City and thence to
Leicester: a distance of 97½ miles
covered in 134 minutes at an average
speed of 43.6 miles per hour – the
longest non-stop run in the world at
that time.

The public marvelled at this new
and unique main-line terminus and a
wag, on seeing St Pancras for the first
time, remarked that it formed 'a

gigantic memorial to Dan Leno' – a
famous music-hall artist of the time,
whose old house at 4 Eve Court, Agar
Town, was one of those swept away to
produce the grandeur that was now St
Pancras station.

Over the years St Pancras has seen
many improvements from its initial
two main-line services dividing at
Trent, one running via Matlock to
Manchester and Liverpool, the other
going north through Chesterfield to
Leeds and Bradford; with the opening
of the Midland's Settle and Carlisle
line this latter train was extended to
Scotland.

In 1872 the Midland opened all its
trains to third class passengers and
then announced in October 1874 that
from the following January it was to
abolish second class accommodation
altogether. This displeased both its
rivals, and even other companies not
in direct competition, as it put pressure
on them to do likewise.

A little earlier, after a trial run from
St Pancras to Bedford, with a lunch
served en route, the Midland had
introduced the British public to the
luxury of Mr Pullman's bogie parlour
cars and convertible sleeping carriages,

with a smoothness of ride not previously experienced in the normal six-wheeled vehicles of the period which were still used almost exclusively by all the other companies.

In 1874 some eighteen Midland and six Great Eastern trains left St Pancras on a weekday, and these were joined by a further fifty-nine trains from Farringdon Street and fourteen working through from the London, Chatham & Dover line. Here was a considerable traffic to be dealt with on the lines north of St Pancras. The Great Eastern services began on 1 August 1870 and their trains worked in from Cambridge via Tottenham North Junction and Kentish Town by an agreement which gave the Midland access via Stratford to London Docks.

Until the mid 1880s St Pancras continued to improve its services to all parts, so much so that Edward Foxwell, writing in 1883, commented: 'This line is to be admired for the uniform excellence and symmetrical running of its trains, the roominess of its carriages and the energy with which it has developed "through" services.' By way of illustration he cited the 5.15 a.m. newspaper train from St Pancras which reached Bedford 'easily in the hour', a distance of 49¾ miles, 'and

then does the next 49½ miles to Leicester in the next hour. These are the sort of things that do not happen out of England.'

The station was damaged by bombs on the night of 17 February 1918, when twenty people were killed and thirty-three injured, and again during the Second World War when the station was closed for two periods of several days although casualties were not so serious.

After the First World War railways in general went into a decline from which they were never to recover; neither the Midland itself nor St Pancras was ever to return to those halcyon days before hostilities began. Only 8465 private motor cars had been in existence in 1904, rising to 132,015 by the outbreak of the war; by 1921 this number had grown to 314,769. Goods vehicles increased from 4000 in 1904 to 82,000 by 1914 and to a staggering 151,000 by 1922. The Midland, like other companies, was slow to realize what this meant to their traffic and as these events were followed by post-war recession, labour troubles in the coal industry and a general strike in 1926, their effects were to be both devastating and far-reaching.

Below
The train shed in use with an interesting variety of stock and a Midland train in the centre foreground. On the right stands a Great Eastern train.

Top
A pair of expresses ready to depart – on
the left is class 3 4-4-0 738, while to the
right class 2 4-4-0 411 and oil-burning class
3 768 double-head a second train in this
view taken in July 1921.

Centre
Kirtley 2-4-0 No. 15 runs into St Pancras
with a Tilbury line train in early LMS days.

Bottom
St Pancras in 1919 with Johnson 4-4-2 625
having just arrived. Note the variety of
hoardings and the water hand-pump for
charging the carriage-roof water tanks on
the extreme left.

Midland main-line passenger services were remodelled and some half a dozen crack long-distance trains, including a 10.45 a.m. from St Pancras to Glasgow, a 2.05 p.m. to Manchester, with a journey time of 4½ hours, and a reciprocal service from Glasgow to St Pancras were inaugurated. Motive power for these was usually the ubiquitous and stalwart Midland Compound 4-4-0s (introduced by Johnson in 1901 and further developed by Deeley), building of which continued well into LMS days.

The Midland Grand Hotel finally closed its doors under London Midland terminus. In 1872, for instance, some 171,000 passengers and 746 season tickets were booked at the station, rising to 652,378 and 2028 season tickets at the turn of the century; by the close of the Midland era in 1922, 1,028,010 passengers were booked on the route with some 2534 season tickets in addition.

The Midland Grand Hotel closed finally its doors under London Midland & Scottish Railway ownership in April 1935, largely as a result of rising operating costs and falling receipts, mainly because of its lack of bathrooms and washing facilities. Today the building remains in use purely as office accommodation and as the head-quarters of the British Transport Hotels Group. The station emerged from the Second World War in bad repair and was re-glazed in a different style from the Barlow original.

St Pancras and the Midland lines, along with the remainder of the LMS network, passed into the hands of the nation on 1 January 1948 and became part of British Railways. A bold sug-gestion in the 'Administrative County of London Development Plan 1951' was the electrification of the line out as far as St Albans or even Luton; in the event there was little immediate change until 18 January 1960, when a new service of diesel multiple-unit trains was introduced between St Pancras and Bedford as part of the BR modernization plans of the late 1950s.

Top
Samuel Johnson's magnificently turned out 4-2-2 2601 'Princess of Wales' stands ready for departure about 1901. This locomotive won the Grand Prix for the Midland at the Paris Exhibition of 1900.

Bottom
An old poster advertising the introduction of dining carriages between St Pancras and Glasgow (St Enoch) which took place on 1 July 1893.

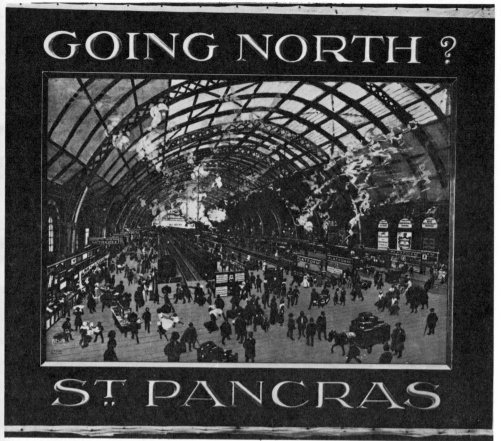

In the summer of 1963 a platform barrier screen, some 240 feet long, was erected right across the concourse at the end of the tracks and the former open view of all platforms was gone for ever.

In 1960 a novel service was introduced in the form of a diesel-electric-powered 'Midland Pullman' train running from Manchester to London at 8.50 in the morning and back the same evening at 6.10, taking just 3 hours 10 minutes, and stopping only at Cheadle Heath. First class only and subject to £1 supplement, the service was intended to provide a businessmen's train from Manchester to the capital while the electrification of the West Coast main line out of Euston took place. Later a mid-day trip to Leicester, Loughborough and Nottingham and back was introduced, but as soon as the electrification work was completed to Manchester the train made its last trip, on 15 April 1966.

In 1961 the magnificent Midland line to Manchester between Matlock and Chinley lost all its services to stations between these points and closure soon followed. There was even talk that St Pancras might be closed as a main-line station and its services re-routed to Euston. However the threat passed. St Pancras has recently been the subject of a BR modernization plan. The whole interior has been redecorated and the booking hall and enquiry office arrangement modernized but it still retains the use of the magnificent carved wooden booking-

Above
One of the famous posters advertising St Pancras painted by Fred Taylor for the Midland in 1910. This is the original canvas.

Below
This photograph, which abounds with period flavour, depicts the booking hall at St Pancras as it was on 4 January 1912 at 12.30 p.m. Note the destination board, the advertising and the original booking-office screen, now moved to a new site to the left of the hall, as seen here.

Top
Johnson 4-2-2 1856 stands at Cambridge Street loco sidings awaiting her turn of duty in about 1897.

Centre
Deeley 0-6-4T 2013 departing from platform 7 with a local train in about 1928.

Bottom
This fine study of Midland compounds 1027 and 1045 in pristine condition typifies the period when they were the mainstay of express motive power on the Midland lines in the 1920s and early 1930s.

Top
A further study of a compound 4-4-0, this time in 1947 when wartime had taken its toll and standards of cleanliness had definitely slipped.

Centre
Midland & London, Brighton & South Coast Railways inter-station motor bus running between St Pancras, Charing Cross and Victoria. Parties of four or more with tickets between Midland stations over 100 miles from London travelled free of charge.

Bottom
Compound 4-4-0 1030 arriving with an express from Manchester early in 1912. The unusual double signal box at St Pancras can be seen on the left.

A London inter-station bus of 1905, operated by the Midland Railway.

office screen which has been refurbished and relocated on the opposite wall of the old booking hall facing the other way.

But that is not all – the main line (between Bedford and St Pancras) has been electrified on the 25kV overhead system and a brand new range of electric multiple unit rolling stock built to replace the worn-out diesel railcars of the 1950s and 1960s. The complete length was made live on 27 September 1982 with the switching on of the Kentish Town–St Pancras section. At the time of writing the old diesel units still battle on, awaiting finalization of new manning agreements with the railway unions for the new stock.

To crown it all, on 1 October 1982 a new service of High Speed Trains began to run to St Pancras from South Yorkshire and the East Midlands, significantly cutting journey times. So

Top
A double-headed train gets under way, hauled by Johnson 4-2-2 79 and a Belpaire boilered class 3 4-4-0 857, in about 1908.

Centre
Kirtley 0-4-4T 1208 at work as station pilot at St Pancras in 1930.

Bottom
Midland compound 1097 makes a spectacular start with the 9.15 p.m. night sleeper for Edinburgh (Waverley) in the late 1920s; to the right a Kirtley 0-4-4T, like the one above, awaits her next duties.

St Pancras enjoys a somewhat un-expected new lease of life, which it is to be hoped will see it on its way in good heart into the 1990s and beyond.

And who was St Pancras?

He was a boy born about AD 290 in Asia Minor, orphaned before his teens, who went to live at his uncle's villa near Rome. In 303 the notorious Emperor Diocletian launched his wave of persecution against those of the Christian faith; during the massacres the boy and his uncle were converted to the faith. In the following year the boy was challenged to abandon his new religion, and when he refused he was led out of the city to the Aurelian Way and put to death by the sword – at the age of fourteen. He was later declared a saint by the Roman Catholic Church and has his saint's day on 12 May.

Top
The dreaming spires of St Pancras as seen in 1983 across the site of Somers Town goods depot.

Centre
The Railway Cafe & Restaurant beneath St Pancras station on St Pancras Road, largely unaltered since it was built in 1866.

Bottom
Class 2P 4-4-0 40420, piloting Jubilee 45627 'Sierra Leone', runs into the station past the inevitable group of train-spotters in the early 1950s.

3
To the
City of Martyrs-
St Albans

Leaving the magnificent train shed of St Pancras behind, the passenger route to the north threads its way past innumerable junctions, points and crossovers, and in a little over nine miles has passed the locations of no fewer than nine former Midland stations, four of which no longer survive. To the left lie the remains of the Somers Town and St Pancras goods depots and just beyond the overbridge (which carries the former North London Railway line to Broad Street, to which the Midland had access via a fiercely graded incline) stands St Paul's Road Junction on the right. From here, by means of a tunnel, the Midland gained access to the Metropolitan and Moorgate Street.

Beyond a short tunnel lies the site of the first suburban station at Camden Road, which once served the local populace in the area but was a casualty of the First World War, and closed on 1 January 1916.

Kentish Town, the next station (still surviving), stands only a quarter of a mile to the north and was the place where locomotives were changed for the condensing type which consumed their own exhaust steam; this enabled them to work over the Metropolitan underground lines to Moorgate Street via its sulphurous ever-smoking tunnels. Also from here ran a daily service to Victoria on the South Eastern & Chatham, with thirteen trains daily. Expresses formerly called here, and in 1868 the longest non-stop run in the country was from here to Leicester: 97½ miles covered in 2 hours and 14 minutes at an average speed of 43.6 miles per hour.

Top
Driver's nightmare at night – the signal gantry at St Pancras in about 1890, with the Somers Town goods yard branch to the right.

Centre
Somers Town milk and fish depot, seen here, was the Midland's chief distribution centre for London. This view was taken by the Midland's own photographer on a visit in 1894. The whole of this depot has now been swept away.

Bottom
The entrance to the tunnel leading to Moorgate Street as it was in August 1953.

Top
Camden Town High Street in about 1906
with a horse bus and a variety of cabs and
carts. Pond's Coffee House, with its dining
rooms, was a popular meeting place for
Edwardians, while the moneylender was
less frequently resorted to than the ever-
popular pawnbroker.

Centre
Rare view of Camden Road Midland
station which closed on 1 January 1916.

Bottom
Work in hand on the widening of the
Camden Road station cutting to permit
fast, slow and goods lines to run alongside
each other.

To the north of the station stood a large locomotive depot, opened with the line to service and maintain a fleet of locomotives required to work the traffic of the area. The sheds were of roundhouse pattern, with lines for stabling locomotives radiating from a central turntable. The depot also had a large repair shop, second only in size to that at Derby, as well as a paint shop; it was also the district locomotive superintendent's domain and headquarters. The most famous of these superintendents was Robert Weatherburn, whose father had also been a railwayman, starting on the Leicester & Swannington Railway in April 1832. Robert was born in January 1841 and was brought up to 'follow in father's footsteps' (as the song has it). In June 1885 he became locomotive foreman at Kentish Town, where he remained until his retirement in January 1896, having reached the age limit of 65 years. Railways in Victorian days, and even in the early part of this century, were a family concern and the Midland was no exception.

At the depot some of the paint-shop staff developed a passion for occasionally adding extra embellishments to the paintwork of repaired locomotives, while cleaning staff of the running shed added their own little touches by working up fantastic overlapping patterns in the film of oil and grease on the larger areas of the engine or its tender.

Top
Beyer Peacock 4-4-0 tank locomotive 205, seen here on Kentish Town locomotive depot, was one of six specially provided to work the services to Moorgate Street for which she sports the condensing apparatus to minimize exhaust steam.

Centre
Robert Weatherburn, District Locomotive Superintendent of the Midland, seen here in his office at the Kentish Town depot.

Bottom
Kentish Town paint shop on 15 June 1903 with a pair of 0-6-0 tank locomotives, Nos. 1379 and 1380, and a Johnson single-wheeler receiving attention.

Kentish Town station is being rebuilt and modernized to fit it for the next generation of electric trains, and continues to play host to the thousands of commuters in a never-ending stream of trains which carry them into St Pancras each morning, and happily home to their families after the day's work is done. The station was closed for goods purposes on 2 August 1971.

After Kentish Town a branch line diverged to the left and then passed over the main line to South Tottenham (once part of the Tottenham & Hampstead Junction Company's line of 1862), which enabled the Midland to join up with the Great Eastern, to Tottenham and Forest Gate, in 1894, by means of an extension from South Tottenham to Woodgrange Park, it joined the Tilbury and Southend lines. By using this route the Midland were able, from 1899, to run trains directly to and from Tilbury Docks (to serve passenger liners using the Orient Line to and from Australia) and to travel directly to St Pancras without the fuss of crossing London. The London, Tilbury and Southend line was absorbed into the Midland in 1912. By this means also the Great Eastern Company was able to run trains directly into St Pancras from its Cambridge main line by means of running powers; these services commenced on 1 August 1870, while a direct link was also established with the London & North Western Company's Hampstead line near Gospel Oak.

The next station was once Haverstock Hill, built where the line is about to enter Belsize Tunnel, and serving the local population on the eastern edge of Belsize Park in the Haverstock Hill and Gospel Oak suburbs. This two-platform station was a First World War casualty, and closed on 1 January 1916.

The line now plunges into the depths of Belsize Tunnel, 1 mile 107 yards long on the goods lines, 1 mile 11 yards long on the passenger lines

Top
A 'down' passenger train at Kentish Town about 1905 in the care of Kirtley 2-4-0 No. 826A.

Centre
Kentish Town station during the widening of the line in 1904–5.

Bottom
The top of Hampstead High Street as it was before 1886, when many of the shops and houses seen here were demolished to make road improvements.

40

and running under Haverstock Hill and Belsize Park (in former days the home of Lord Wotton and later Lord Chesterfield). 'Old Belsize', as the house was called, became a place of public amusement in 1720 during the reign of the first two Georges, and in order to protect patrons from the unwelcome attentions of thugs, highwaymen and ruffians, the proprietor engaged 'twelve stout fellows completely armed' to patrol the road between Belsize and London.

The proprietor, a Mr Howell, offered a variety of amusements such as carp fishing, stag hunts in the grounds and gambling. Refreshments included tea, chocolate, ratafia and a large variety of wines to accompany the fish, pasties, venison pies and other delicacies. The number of stout guards was increased to thirty and the popularity of the venue was increased by the patronage of the Prince and Princess of Wales; later events attracted some three to four hundred road coaches!

In the later years the house came into the ownership of the Hon. Spencer Perceval, who was assassinated in the lobby of the House of Commons in 1812; Old Belsize fell into disrepair. It was pulled down in 1852, and the property and land were surrendered to housing development. Within thirty years the whole estate was submerged beneath a sea of suburban dwellings, save for a single avenue of noble elms.

As recorded in chapter 1, the Midland Board had wisely decided that traffic to London was likely to grow at a good rate and had therefore purchased sufficient land to enable four tracks to be laid from Bedford to London; four tracks were actually laid from Welsh Harp Junction to St Pancras goods station from the outset.

Top
West End & Brondesbury looking south, with a '115' class 4-2-2 on a 'down' express, probably in the summer of 1905. The goods lines are on the right and the local lines, which were opened on 3 December 1905, are on the left.

Centre
Ladies clad in the modest Edwardian one-piece bathing suits are the focus of attention in this 1907 view of Hampstead Pool.

Bottom
The famous fair on Hampstead Heath and the stalls which supplied 'food and drinks to suit every taste for one penny'.

41

At Belsize Tunnel, however, to save costs on this enormous engineering task, the Midland employed the unusual arrangement of laying down four sets of lines a few inches apart and intersecting with each other through the tunnel. This avoided having complex junctions at each end of the tunnel, while traffic could be safely regulated to pass through. It was not until 3 February 1884, when the second bore of the tunnel came into use, that this arrangement was dispensed with.

Emerging from the tunnel, the line next arrived at Finchley Road station, which was constructed adjacent to that thoroughfare and provided the new tenants on the western edge of the former park and neighbouring St John's Wood with a suburban service into the heart of the city. The two-platform station replaced an earlier one which had closed on 3 February 1884, and was itself closed on 11 July 1927.

Passing underneath the LNWR tracks from Willesden to Camden Town, the line arrived at West End station, opened somewhat later than the other. The first train called there on 1 March 1871 to serve the newly established suburban dwellers in the housing around the hamlet of West End set around a triangular village green. The name of the station was changed to West End & Brondesbury on 1 April 1904, and on 1 September 1905 was changed yet again to West Hampstead. Yet another change took place on 1 July 1950 when it became West Hampstead, Midland for goods purposes, and passenger timetables used the new name from 25 September of that year. It still remains open for suburban passenger services.

Beyond this station the railway is surrounded by cemeteries; those of Kilburn and Hampstead lie near the line, while to the east is the Highgate cemetery, last resting-place of many famous people.

Travellers passing through Highgate in former times used to swear by oath

Top
Tennis picnic party on Parliament Hill Fields on August Bank Holiday 1904. Note the gorgeous hats.

Centre
The Bull and Bush hotel, Hampstead presided over by mine host Fred Vinall and made famous by Florrie Forde in the music-hall song.

Bottom
The 5.10 pm 'down' train passing Cricklewood on 6 June 1903 in the care of 2-4-0 No. 151A.

M. R. Child's Hill Running Sheds.

'never to eat brown bread if they could get white nor drink small beer if they could get strong unless they liked the other better'. The covenant, known as 'swearing on the horns', was a flexible one, usually entered into during refreshment at a local inn.

Hampstead itself remains a place of character and charm despite developments over the years. Originally 'Heamstede' (or 'place for a home') and given to Westminster Abbey in AD 986, it had a succession of owners culminating in the Maryon-Wilson family who sold the land to the Metropolitan Board of Works in 1870 for £47,000; two years later some 240 acres of the estate were dedicated to the use of the public.

Hampstead as a village became popular in the eighteenth century as a pleasure resort and a centre for taking the curative waters of the chalybeate spring. Crowds flocked to the village, which grew rapidly as a result; it became the favourite haunt of writers and painters – Dr Johnson, Keats, Romney, Constable, H. G. Wells, Stanley Spencer and Kate Greenaway all resided here at some time.

Following development of Regent's Park and the arrival of the Midland and other railways, urbanization began and between 1829 and 1871 significant changes took place as the population of central London began to spread into the suburbs. In 1900 Hampstead Heath, now preserved as a public open space, marked the beginning of the countryside. It was much frequented by the public, who travelled to places such as the Hampstead garden taverns – The Old Bull and Bush, Jack Straw's Castle, or the assembly and card rooms of the Holly Bush Tavern; alternatively they would take the air on the Heath, where perhaps one of the regular fairs might be in full swing; a fine Whit Monday attracted as many as 50,000 people.

Top
Interior of the Child's Hill running sheds showing the Midland style of radial stabling lines around a central turntable. The depot was later renamed 'Cricklewood'.

Centre
The quaint little 0-4-2 tank, built originally for the Little North Western Railway in 1851 and rebuilt at Derby; it worked the Cricklewood to Gunnersbury local services from 1885 to 1887 and later became a shunting engine at Hendon.

Bottom
The Boys' Brigade on parade in Cricklewood Lane outside the Church Institute about 1905.

The Hampstead Tube was opened by Lloyd George in June 1907 and the surrounding areas (particularly Golders Green, a place of green fields, farm buildings and small cottages around the White Swan public house) soon came under intensive development, leaving the Heath an isolated but important 'lung' for the surrounding suburbs. The nearby suburbs of Child's Hill and Cricklewood, with a station that bore their names jointly until 1 May 1903, also came under development.

At this point on the Midland main line a branch diverged on the left, leading to Acton Wells Junction. Built by the Midland & South Western Junction Railway Company under an act of 1864, this line was some 3¾ miles long and was always worked by the Midland, which absorbed the original company in 1874. This link afforded the Midland an important connection with both the Great Western and London & South Western Companies; the latter was given running powers to the Midland's own extensive sidings at Brent, where the northern end of the triangle joined the main Midland line. In return, the Midland ran over L & SWR metals from Kew Junction to Clapham Junction and, by means of the Metropolitan's Hammersmith Junction

Below
Cricklewood sidings for the sorting of goods traffic as it appeared in March 1905. The locomotive depot can be seen in the background.

line, had access to its own depots for coal, goods and cattle traffic at West Kensington and at Kensington High Street (for coal); these facilities were opened in March 1878.

The Midland purchased some 150 acres of land at Cricklewood for its Locomotive Department to erect an extensive motive power depot, and for the operation of an extensive marshalling yard to service traffic from the various lines in the London area with which the Midland had connections.

The locomotive depot began in 1882 with a large roundhouse to take the place of a small shed at Hendon, which was built in 1870 and could house only four locomotives. With the growth of the sidings at Brent, a second roundhouse was built in 1893 to house and service the increasing number of engines required to work the traffic. Repair shops were also built but were closed and rented out in the 1920s. The depot closed to steam on 14 December 1964.

Goods traffic (latterly worked by diesel locomotives, of course) ceased at Cricklewood station on 6 October 1969, but that station has been completely modernized and continues to provide an important intermediate stopping point on the outer suburban services to Luton and Bedford, about to change from diesel railcar to electric multiple unit. Inside the triangular junction and beyond it extended the massive goods sidings for receiving and despatching coal and minerals as well as other goods. It was

to here that the massive 2-6-6-2 Beyer Garratt locomotives of the LMS hauled their enormous loads of coal from the sorting sidings at Toton in the Notts and Derby coalfields for onward transmission to all points south.

The next station was once the lyrical-sounding Welsh Harp, a single-island platform constructed between the slow lines, which opened with Child's Hill and Cricklewood on 2 May 1870 to serve not only the needs of local commuters but also, more importantly perhaps, the recreational needs of the Victorian working classes and the London holiday-makers who flocked to the nearby inn, The Old Welsh Harp, situated alongside the large Brent Reservoir at Welsh Harp. The reservoir had been built in 1838 to supply water to the Grand Union Canal and was filled by the Brent and Lith rivers. It was a favourite spot for fishing and boating enthusiasts alike, and during the summer a venue for regular Saturday afternoon regattas. Mine host at the tavern no doubt benefited considerably from the influx of summer visitors. However, there was an added bonus for him in winter for, provided the weather was sufficiently frosty, he derived a considerable supplementary income from skaters who flocked to avail themselves of the facilities at a fee of one shilling per person per session. It is on record that in times of hard frost the proprietor raised as much as £1000 per day from this activity!

However, despite all this, the station itself lasted a mere thirty-three years – no doubt times and habits changed – and it closed completely on 30 June 1903. In later years across the waters of the reservoir rose the twin towers of Wembley Stadium, a modern-day Colosseum where sporting contests, less bloody than those of ancient Rome, attract supporters.

"THE JOLLIEST PLACE THAT'S OUT."
SUNG BY
★ MISS ANNIE ADAMS ★
_____

Now, if you want a change, I'll tell you what to do,
Just take a 'bus from Turnham's, and bid London
                                    smoke adieu,
On the pleasures of the rural spot – I have a word to say,
Where anyone, who's fond of fun, can spend a jolly day.

CHORUS:–

Warner's Welsh Harp! – 'Have you ever been there?
Picnics, such tricks! ev'ry day are seen there,
You couldn't find its equal, if you walked for miles
                                    about,
There's no mistake about it – it's the Jolliest Place
                                    That's Out.

There's a Lake, with Boats and Wherries – wherry
                            nice for one who rows,
An Archery Ground, where single girls can always meet
                                    with beaux;
An Ordinary for those who a Good Dinner may desire,
And, they only Charge a Shilling! – which the visitors
                                    admire.

Chorus.

There are Billiard Tables quite as good, as any here in
                                    Town
With many Games that knock *you* up, and Skittles *you*
                                    knock *down;*
There's Tea for those who wish it – you can have it on
                                    the Lawns,
With the sweetest bread and butter – oh! and such
                            delicious Prawns.

Chorus.

There are Lovers' Walks, beneath the trees, where
                            silence aids the charm,
For mooney, yes, and spooney folks to linger, arm
                                    in arm;
Punts for those who Angle, and sit silent as a church,
Good worthy *souls,* who use the *place,* and seldom miss
                                    their *perch.*

Chorus.

But, to tell you all its many charms, 'twould take I'm
                            sure all night,
You'd better go yourselves and see, 'twill fill you with
                                    delight;
Just slip away, some leisure day, and give the Host a call,
At Warner's Famous Paradise, there's Welcome for
                                    you all.

Chorus.

Above
An Edwardian song in praise of Warner's Old Welsh Harp tavern, which is self-explanatory.

Top right
View of The Old Welsh Harp about 1903. The postcard message on the reverse side reads: 'We have just had tea here. Rather a nice place.'

Centre
Johnson single-wheeler 120 heads the 'down' Scotch Express past Welsh Harp station about 1900.

Bottom
Midland period scene typified in this study of a Johnson '2581' class 4-4-0 with an express on the 'up' fast line passing Welsh Harp.

45

Half a mile or so further on is the station of Hendon, from which the Midland commenced a through service on 1 July 1875 via St Paul's Road Junction to the Metropolitan at Farringdon Street and thence all the way to the London Chatham & Dover Railway Company's Victoria Station, an important cross-city link. Hendon was also the receiving point for through LSWR carriages from Portsmouth and Southampton to Manchester and Leeds arriving via Acton Wells Junction, as mentioned previously. An LSWR locomotive worked the stock to Hendon, whence it was worked forward on the slow lines, crossing to the fast line at Elstree.

Hendon marked the end of the major through traffic direct from the North and the point from which distribution of the different traffic towards London took place by various routes. Here arrived heavily loaded passenger trains, continuing towards St Pancras, except for the suburban services, some of which were routed elsewhere; also meat, fish, vegetables, milk, timber, coal, iron and general goods of all kinds, to be sorted for onward transmission to London.

Brent sidings (mentioned previously) provided the means of sorting the goods and mineral traffic and other merchandise for various destinations, and much traffic travelled over the Dudding Hill loop, opened on 1 October 1868. This followed closely upon the opening of the main line on the previous 13 July, the date of opening of the original Hendon

Top
The Great Frost of 1895 enabled this four-in-hand to take to the ice on the Welsh Harp Reservoir at Hendon in February.

Centre
Brent Street, Hendon as it was in 1906, with a group of boys showing interest in the photographer at work.

Bottom
Showing all the neglect of the last days of steam, Jubilee class 4-6-0 45564 'New South Wales' heads an 'up' express through Hendon about 1960.

Station. Hendon lost its goods traffic (with the exception of private siding accommodation) on 1 January 1968 but remains now a much modernized station and an important intermediate stopping point for the regular commuter services to and from the City.

Hendon itself, lying one mile to the south-west, was once a picturesque village with an ancient ivy-covered parish church. In the churchyard stands the gravestone of Robert Thomas Crossfield, a Yorkshire doctor, who died on 8 November 1802, and in whose tribute is inscribed the following epitaph:

Beneath this stone Tom Crossfield lies
He cares not now who laughs or cries
He laughed when sober, but when mellow
Was a harem-scarem brainless fellow
He gave to none designed offence
So 'Honi soit qui mal y pense'

Hendon, once abounding in 'pretty field paths, quiet shady lanes and with hedges full of hawthorns, wild roses, honeysuckles and brambles and bluebells and arums', began to be 'improved' with the coming of the railway. Its rural character soon disappeared amid a great many villas and cottage residences, and Hendon became similar to many other new suburban dormitory villages whose individual characters became blurred and often completely obscured by such intrusion. To the north of the old village a large, government-sponsored housing scheme caused further expansion in the early 1930s, but relieved the appalling slum housing conditions in central London.

Top
Celebrating the Diamond Jubilee of 1897, the inhabitants of Hendon gather on Sunny Hill Fields for a fête and gala day.

Centre
London & South Western Railway 4-4-0 No. 463 stands at Hendon in about 1904, having brought the through coaches from Portsmouth and Southampton to join the Midland express here.

Bottom
Intrepid aeronaut dangles from an early airship over Hendon Aerodrome while a Midland dining car express, hauled by a class 3 4-4-0 No. 773, passes beneath him.

Sitting in his car near Hendon church one day, shortly after his return from an American flying tour, the early English aviator Graham White looked over the expanse of ground before him and decided to buy it. This was in December 1910 and within the year he had established an aerodrome and was giving flying displays. Early biplanes and monoplanes flew wing-tip to wing-tip round the marker pylons and thrilled the public; by 1914 some 60,000 spectators flocked to see the start and finish of the Aerial Derby. The annual Royal Air Force Pageant followed in 1920 and the field was later used as an RAF training ground. Today Hendon is aptly the home of the Royal Air Force Museum.

A mile north of Hendon the goods lines pass over the fast tracks to join with the local passenger lines at Silkstream Junction, named after a nearby stream. Two miles beyond Hendon the Great Northern Railway branch from Finchley to Edgware passes beneath the Midland main line, while away to the left are the hills of Harrow with its famous school.

At Mill Hill, served by the next station, stands a less ancient but no less important public shool founded in 1807 by Nonconformists, driven to take this step by the refusal of established public schools to accept their sons. The school became famous under Dr Weymouth, and many eminent men received their schooling there. Opened as Mill Hill, the station became Mill Hill Broadway on 1 July 1950 for goods purposes and from 25 September 1950 for passenger services. Goods traffic was terminated on 3 August 1964, but the station remains an important intermediate stopping point for suburban passenger services.

Top left
Johnson singles 175, and possibly 27, at the head of a 'down' express, composed of a great variety of stock including a Pullman sleeping car, north of Hendon in about 1900.

Centre left
Idyllic country scene on Highwood Hill with The Plough Inn on the left, in about 1900 before Mill Hill was built up.

Bottom left
A still smart Mill Hill station with typical Midland features is scarcely disturbed by the passing of 'The Palatine' express hauled by Jubilee class 4-6-0 45628 'Somaliland'.

Top right
The Graham White factory at Hendon with biplanes in full production during the First World War, in 1918.

Bottom right
Beauty in motion – Johnson single 145 with a 'down' train near Mill Hill. A Pullman sleeping car is the first vehicle in the train.

Initially opened on 13 July 1868, with the rest of the line, Elstree station was modernized in 1959 with a new booking office, booking hall, enquiry office, left-luggage office and staff mess room. There is also a brand-new entrance on the Shenley Road to serve the new Borehamwood housing estates on that side of the line. A new footbridge was provided to link the new facilities to the old side of the station; the work was carried out by Messrs Trollope and Colls Ltd. At the same time, in conjunction with the Hertfordshire County Council, improvements were made to the roads and roadbridge to fit the station for its modern role.

At the time the Midland arrived (less than a year after the Edgware, Highgate & London Railway opened on 23 September 1867) the village of Mill Hill straggled for a distance of about a mile along the summit of the hill which was a favoured dwelling place of the well-to-do, with fine elm trees lining both sides of the main road. Sir Stamford Raffles, founder of Singapore and of the Zoological Society, spent his last few years here in a 'house, small but compact', with 112 acres of grassland, while his next-door neighbour was the renowned William Wilberforce. Since those times the whole neighbourhood has been swallowed up in the ever-extending suburban development of the 1920s.

Elstree Tunnels, 1050 yards long on the fast lines and 1058 yards long on the slow, run through Woodcock Hill and bring the traveller into Hertfordshire and to Elstree itself. Some ten miles from London, with a station three quarters of a mile from the old village and right next to the old hamlet of Boreham Wood, Elstree stands in four parishes and two counties – Hertfordshire and Middlesex.

A derivation of 'Eaglestree' (or more probably 'Eald Street', standing as it does on Watling Street), the village stands on elevated ground near to the Roman station of Sullonicae. The manor was granted by King Offa to St Albans Abbey, and later passed to the Earls of Strafford. Standing in an elevated position, with views of St Albans, it was described in the 1870s as 'quiet, clean and cheerful with an air of old-fashioned rural comfort'. Today the hamlet has grown to embrace (or perhaps to be embraced by) Boreham Wood, now an extensive suburban conurbation. The station, opened with the line as Elstree, became Elstree & Boreham Wood on 1 June 1869; it reverted to its former name on 1 April 1904; became Elstree & Borehamwood on 21 September 1953, and finally reverted to Elstree again on 6 May 1974!

Elstree has had many famous sons and daughters; numbered among them are Sir Richard Burton, the explorer, William Macready, the actor, and Martha Reay, the daughter of an Elstree labourer and mistress of the Earl of Sandwich, who was killed while leaving Covent Garden Theatre by the Reverend Hackman – duly hanged at Tyburn gallows for his crime eleven days later.

Elstree is, of course, celebrated for its film studios, opened there in 1908 by J. D. Williams, who appointed Herbert Wilcox as director-in-chief. The first British 'talkie', *Blackmail*, was made here in 1929. Metro-Goldwyn-Meyer also had studios at Borehamwood, where the classic film *Goodbye Mr Chips*, starring Robert Donat, was made. The Korda brothers, Frank Launder (of Hitchin) and Sidney Gilliatt worked here, producing the St Trinian's comedies. The MGM studios closed in 1970, but Associated British Pictures (as EMI) continued to use the studios for television series; *The Avengers* was made here as well as the films *The Dambusters* and *Moby Dick*.

The county of Hertfordshire has many features of interest, and Camden writes that there was 'scarce one in

Top
Elstree station, looking north with a local train in the 'down' slow platform. The photograph dates from about 1906.

Bottom
Elstree High Street still retains some rustic charm with its board-faced cottages and the inevitable group of curious children.

50

England that could show more traces of antiquity'. Indeed, the competition for land in this county grew so keen that a common saying was 'He who buys land in Hertfordshire pays two years purchase for the air'. Silk and cotton were both manufactured here in earlier times, and turnips were first introduced into the county by a farmer who received £100 from Oliver Cromwell himself for his enterprise. Wheat was once such a fine crop in this area that it has given its name to Wheathampstead on the river Lea.

Today the county, at least at its southern end, is largely commuter territory for thousands travelling into and out of London daily by car, bus and train. Yet much agriculture remains despite the poor stony soil, and in some parts enclosed fields have now given way to modern farming of larger areas. Wheat is grown in the west, barley in the north and east and hay in the south. From these crops came straw plaiting, and malt for brewing from the barley.

The local dialect has its charms as well as its ancient traditions, which distinguish the villager from the new commuter types, who may well not understand 'It's a fraasty ole mornin' maaster' or 'Oi ent gawt toime ter stan' 'ere a-chattin'. Describing a shrub, a villager once explained, 'That be rosemary. They do say it only grows where the missus is maaster, an it do grow 'ere loike woild foire!' Local delicacies include 'aarb tea' made from agrimony, camomile or yarrow leaves; gooseberry pudding (after which the first Sunday in July is traditionally named); and watercress soup, made from boiled potato and leek liquid with chopped cress added and a little cream. Such were the charms of old Hertfordshire which the Midland had invaded with its new line, and by its coming and the other transport forms that followed, the county was surely changed more in a century than in the previous thousand years.

Top
The prototype Fowler 2-6-4 tank locomotive 42300 bursts out of the slow line tunnel at Elstree with a 'down' local train on 11 August 1953.

Centre
A 'down' express, consisting of Bain coaching stock, near Elstree in 1907 hauled by Johnson Class 3 4-4-0 No. 716.

Bottom
One of the huge Beyer Garratt 2-6-6-2 locomotives (47984) heads a heavy freight train through Elstree station on 27 March 1954.

Next on the route is Radlett station which was only a second-thought name, the original intention being to name it Aldenham, after another village in the area. Radlett was once owned by Walter Phillimore, a wealthy Liberal lord and friend of Gladstone who passed it on to his son, Bobby. He it was who, in the early part of this century, proceeded to put up (according to Bertrand Russell) 'vast numbers of cheap, ugly, sordid suburban villas which brought in an enormous profit', turning it into a commuter centre and dormitory area a mere fifteen minutes or so by train from St Pancras. Almost the entire conurbation is relatively modern and residential by nature.

The local church at Radlett, however, pre-dates this relatively modern development, having been built for the spiritual welfare of the thousands of navvies who toiled to construct the Midland line in 1867–8. The station itself opened with the line and has recently been modernized along with others on the section to Bedford.

Across the river Colne to the left of the line stands a most picturesque residence, with its cedars of Lebanon – Parkbury Lodge, formerly the home of the Marquis of Blandford. Here also now is Radlett aerodrome, once the base of the Handley Page aircraft company founded by Sir Frederick Handley Page at Barking in 1908 and moved to Radlett after the first successful flight of the Handley Page Hannibal (a four-engined biplane airliner) from there in 1930. The company made a significant contribution to the Second World War effort with the Halifax bomber, of which some six thousand were built. After the war the company entered the jet age with the Handley Page Victor bombers and the light Jetstream; in 1962 Sir Frederick died, unaware that by the end of the decade his company would cease to exist.

Napsbury is the next station, opened quite late, on 19 June 1905,

Top
Immaculate Kirtley 2-4-0 No. 58 stands at Radlett station with a local train in about 1916.

Centre
Compound 4-4-0 1044 heads an 'up' Whit Saturday special through Harper Lane Cutting at Radlett on 15 May 1948.

Bottom
The rather uninspiring island platform at Napsbury station with a 'down' local train headed by a 2-6-4 tank in the early 1950s.

comprising only a single-island platform between the 'up' and 'down' slow lines with a siding serving the Middlesex County Asylum. Served only by local trains, eight 'up' (one Wednesdays only) and nine 'down' in 1910 on the St Pancras–Luton service. By 1957 there were only five weekday trains in each direction, and the station closed completely on 14 September 1959.

Almost straight now, the Midland line runs into St Albans, 19¾ miles from St Pancras. Called 'the city of martyrs', St Albans is so steeped in history that there is (recorded one writer) 'scarcely any in all England more full of interest to the antiquary'.

St Albans takes its name from the first British martyr, a high-born citizen of the Roman fortification of Verulam, the site of which is adjacent to the present city. Alban sheltered a persecuted Christian priest and was so impressed that he too embraced the faith. The authorities eventually traced the priest to Alban's house, but he escaped by exchanging cloaks. When Alban was confronted with the deception he boldly affirmed his faith, and after refusing to recant was taken out and beheaded. This was on 22 July 209. Subsequently a shrine was built on or near the spot, but it was not until the late fourth century that a monastic church was built over it. In the eighth century Offa, King of Mercia, founded the abbey and reconstituted the monastery under the rule of St Benedict; the Norman part of the present building replaced Offa's in 1077.

Top
An ex-Miland compound 4-4-0 in full flight with an 'up' special passing Napsbury on 21 July 1950.

Bottom
Work in progress at St Albans in connection with the widening of the main line in the 1880s. The line in the foreground is the Great Northern from Hatfield with its typical somersault signal, and just beyond the Midland overbridge can be seen the original GN London Road station.

At 550 feet, the church is the second longest in Britain, and the magnificent Norman tower, 144 feet high, is built with bricks taken from the Roman town. All the outer buildings of the monastery (except the Great Gateway) were demolished in 1539 and the Abbey was purchased from the Crown for £400 by the townspeople in 1550 to become the parish church. St Albans attained city status in 1875. A recent addition is the beautiful modern Chapter House opened by Her Majesty Queen Elizabeth II accompanied by Prince Philip on 8 July 1982.

St Albans' other claims to fame in former times were the making of gentlemen's straw hats and the growing of watercress. 'When they [watercresses] are in season', said a one-time Victorian stationmaster, 'we send away perhaps two tons or more per night, for months together.' They

Top
'Race to the north' – compound 4-4-0 No. 41050 working the 17.55 Fridays-only express from St Pancras to Derby, overtaking sister loco No. 41009 on the 'down' 17.45 St Pancras to Bedford at Napsbury on 4 August 1950.

Centre
The porte-cochère at St Albans City station as it was on 8 August 1953.

Bottom
Fowler 2-6-2 tank 40024 arrives at St Albans with a 'down' Moorgate train on a clear June evening in 1957. The engine carries the special Moorgate headcode and the carriages are new stock introduced in 1955.

were sent mainly to London and Manchester (via the Midland of course) and were carefully packed in half-hundredweight hampers.

Just to the south of the station lies the Schweppes soft drinks factory. The Verulam golf course, a little further south still, is a favourite haunt of the golfing fraternity, who can be seen in action alongside the line – the railway of course being 'out of bounds'.

The famous people St Albans can boast include Sir Francis Bacon who, as Lord Verulam, is interred in the city's St Michael's Church, and Sarah Jennings, the Duchess of Marlborough, who was born in 1660 at Sandridge some six miles to the north. Of the town's infamous people, none was more renowned and feared than Mother Haggy the local witch who, it was alleged, could turn herself into a lion, a hare or a cat. She survived several attempts to prove her sorcery by ducking her in the river fastened to the witches' ducking-stool.

In former times St Albans had been an important coaching stop on the route from London to Holyhead, but Thomas Telford, improving the appalling state of the roads in the area, cut a new London Road which proved very popular with coach drivers. They

Right
The clock tower is the central feature of this St Albans street scene, dating from about 1905.

Bottom
St Albans Abbey as it was on 27 May 1892 depicted in an official Midland Railway publicity photograph.

would race each other neck and neck all the way from Highgate, to the considerable danger of their passengers, occasionally colliding in the night as they dashed with careless abandon headlong into St Albans.

The London & North Western Railway was first into the town with a line from Watford, opened on 5 May 1858, closely followed by the Hatfield & St Albans Railway Company which in 1863 opened a line between the Great Northern at Hatfield and St Albans where it had its own independent station (later connected by an extension to the LNWR station). This line was later taken over by the Great Northern Company. The Midland was thus last in the field, their station being opened for regular services with the main line to London on 13 July 1868. The station has undergone many changes over the years; it became owned first by the LMS and later by British Railways, and is currently enjoying a renewed lease of life as a modernized intermediate station.

The city still retains many fascinating corners and, while parts are clearly past repair and ready to be re-developed, praiseworthy attempts have been made to preserve the best of the old. However, the city centre has rather poor shopping facilities and suffers from too much traffic; it seems to be on the horns of the usual dilemma – to conserve or to modernize?

Top
The Fighting Cocks Inn at St Albans is claimed to be the oldest inhabited house in the country and was built as a boat-house for the monastery by King Offa in about the year 795.

Centre
A witches' ducking stool or chair, similar perhaps to the one in which Mother Haggy was subjected to her 'trial'. This one is at Fordwick.

Bottom
The White Hart and Holywell Hill at St Albans in about 1920.

4
Into deepest Bedfordshire

Leaving St Albans, the Midland passes through rich, undulating pasture and woodland, past the little village of Sandridge, through Bowling Alley and on to Harpenden. At one time Harpenden was merely a large village to the west of the line, but it has been considerably extended during the twentieth century by modern housing spreading tentacles outwards from its centre.

In this part of the county there were once many water wells, covering an area extending from the London suburbs to the crest of the Chiltern Hills which meet the line south of Bedford. The Chilterns are an outcrop of a chalk mass which dips down under the London basin and appears again as the Kent and Essex downs. Sandwiched as it is between London clay above and gault below, it is fine,

Previous page
Compound 4-4-0 No. 41181 pauses at Harpenden with the 3.20 p.m. St Pancras to Kettering train on 21 March 1957. This was the last regular compound working into St Pancras and it ceased the following month.

Below
40022, a Fowler 2-6-2 tank, waits at Harpenden with the 8.50 a.m. train for Moorgate which comprises Midland stock dating back to 1911.

water-bearing rock, readily yielding a supply wherever the clay shield is penetrated.

At Harpenden the station, opened with the line, was built on the Rothamstead estate, the former home of Sir John Bennet Lawes. He was born, lived, worked and died on his own estate, and in 1843 began chemical experiments in a barn using his fields for testing various types of manure. It was he who introduced artificial fertilizers to the world and later joined up with Sir J. H. Gilbert, working in association with him for fifty-eight years. In 1889 he founded the Lawes Agricultural Trust, endowing it with £100,000 to enable his life's work to continue. His Rothamstead Experimental Station stands on the edge of Harpenden Common, and is an Adam-style building of red brick and white stone resembling a chapel. It was given to Sir John, along with a costly piece of silver plate, by local farmers in 1855 in appreciation of his services to their community.

The village of Harpenden, formerly called Harden, belonged to the De Hoo family in the time of Edward I and its church dates from Norman times. In the village the annual fête took place on the Common on the

Friday before Derby Day and was known as 'The Races'. This event was established by Henry Oldaker, licensee of the Cross Keys, and the races were run annually in May up to the First World War. One writer complained that 'for two days in the year all the London pick-pockets, sharpers, and blackguards who happen to be out of gaol, are permitted to make Harpenden their own, and to make travelling in a first class carriage on the Midland Railway a danger to men and an impossibility to ladies'.

Lady Mary Carbery, who visited 'The Races' as a child with her family, told of maids having their fortunes told by a gypsy while a policeman looked the other way, and of a cheapjack doctor in a top hat and black coat shouting from a cart about his 'mirryaculous cure-all 'ealth pills'.

Straw plaiting, sewing and brewing were once strong local industries in addition, of course, to the primary activity of farming. Today the village has changed out of all recognition, and modern housing estates surround the old centre. St George's co-educational school here was at one time regarded as the foremost of its kind in the country. Among its famous residents Harpenden can count actress Ellen

Terry and a certain Mr Bartholomew, better known as comedian Eric Morecambe.

Harpenden station still survives in modernized form, but is not nearly so attractive as others on this stretch of the line, since little remains of the original Midland-style station, save a much altered and rather unattractive recently renovated station building on the 'down' platform. The station serves commuters on the Bedford–St Pancras services.

A mile north of Harpenden are the remains of Westfield and Ashfield Woods, reminders of the days when the Chiltern Hills were covered with dense forests – the haunts of wild boars, bulls, stags, bears and wolves and a hiding place for robbers and outlaws.

To the right is the river Lea, which gives its name to both Leagrave and Luton, and to the left the trackbed of a branch of the Midland which once ran to Hemel Hempstead, diverging from the main line beneath an overbridge. This was the 'Nicky' line, perhaps so called because of the old Pullman picnic cars used on its trains. Other theories are that it is short for 'knickerbockers', which the navvies wore when constructing the line, a form of dress not seen before in these parts; or is perhaps derived from St Nicholas, through which parish much of the line passes.

Promoted in 1863 by the Hemel Hempstead Railway Company and supported by subsequent Acts, it had powers to construct a line from Boxmoor on the LNWR to Harpenden linking both the Midland and Great Northern lines there. However, the promoters found that in order to succeed, the line would have to be worked by a larger company, and the Midland was approached to take on the traffic operation, which it agreed to do.

Top
Compound 41082 heads the 'up' 9.07 a.m. Bedford to St Pancras past St Albans North on 3 July 1948. Note the Midland signals on the right.

Centre
Nottingham-based compound 4-4-0 No. 1029, in superbly clean condition, runs through Harpenden with an 'up' express on 19 October 1929.

Bottom
Harpenden station in about 1902, with an 'up' train approaching headed by a pair of Johnson 4-2-2's; on the platform lie crates of watercress.

59

The branch was opened with full ceremony on 16 July 1877, the initial service consisting of four trains each way daily, except Sunday, between Hemel Hempstead and Luton calling at Redbourn and Chiltern Green. However, the section from Boxmoor to Hemel Hempstead remained unopened, and in 1886 the small company was dissolved and the line passed into the ownership of the Midland Railway Company. The service to Luton continued until 1888, when the new south curve at Harpenden Junction was opened on 2 July, giving a much improved service to London via Harpenden rather than passengers being forced to go in a northerly direction to Chiltern Green or Luton and then having to retrace their steps.

To work the traffic a variety of motive power was employed, including the diminutive standard Midland 0-6-0, some old Somerset & Dorset 2-4-0 tender locomotives, and a Midland & Great Northern 4-4-0 tank engine coupled to an old Pullman car and a Midland suburban carriage (as a push-pull unit). Also used for a time was one of the Midland steam railmotors, originally built for the Morecambe–Heysham service but displaced upon electrification, while in LMS days a Karrier road-railer bus underwent trials. In later days 2-6-2 tank locomotives were used to work the final period of passenger services over the line.

From July 1914 the branch became

Top
Harpenden High Street as it was in about 1920, significantly empty of all but one cart.

Centre
A happy group of children at the National Children's Home and Orphanage, Harpenden Branch, about 1928. Perhaps the cup is a prize won by the group?

Bottom
The Harpenden Races in progress in about 1911. They were held every year from 1848 until 1914, but never recommenced because of the temporary nature of the grandstand and the Jockey Club's refusal to renew the licence after the war.

one class only and on 16 June 1947 passenger services were 'temporarily' withdrawn, never to be recommenced. Goods services over the line were terminated on 6 July 1964 with the closure of Redbourn sidings, but part of the line was reopened as a private mineral railway by Hemelite Ltd on 30 April 1968 and continues in use today.

Beyond Harpenden Junction the line crosses over the trackbed of the former Hertford, Luton and Dunstable branch of the Great Northern Railway on its northerly course from Welwyn Garden City towards the now demolished Luton Bute Street station.

As the line crosses the Lea it runs into Bedfordshire and reaches the pretty village of New Mill End with the nearby station of Chiltern Green, which obviously takes its name (as does the nearby village) from its proximity to the Chiltern Hills, running from Goring in Oxfordshire through Buckinghamshire to Tring, sometimes as wide as 15 or 20 miles across.

In earlier times, when there were as yet no proper police forces in the land, this once-wild remote region was the home of outlaws, and it was to suppress their activities that the office of 'Steward of the Chiltern Hundreds' was established by the Crown. Today we are perhaps more law-abiding and the area has lost its remoteness, but the office still exists to enable members of the House of Commons to relinquish their seats without resigning from them.

Top
Harpenden Junction with a Johnson 2-4-0 at the head of a train crossing from the fast to the goods lines, which become the slow lines from this point onwards. The Hemel Hempsted (spelt by the Midland without the 'a') branch can be seen diverging to the left.

Centre
Midland 0-6-0 tank 1669 stands at Hemel Hempsted with the branch-line train comprising a brake third and an old steam motor coach.

Bottom
Hemel Hempsted station and, beyond, the Midland Commercial Hotel. The branch train coaches standing in the siding comprise a Pullman parlour car and a third class brake carriage.

Chiltern Green was the station for Luton Hoo and the Great Northern also had a station at this point. On the left is the site of this famous residence, founded in Saxon times and once the home of Sir Robert Napier, who left it unfinished. It passed to John, 3rd Earl of Bute, who reconstructed and improved it. It was destroyed by fire in 1844 and rebuilt by John Shaw Leigh. The present house was built in 1903 for Sir Julius Wernher to the design of Mawes.

The station at Chiltern Green opened with the line on 13 July 1868 but after the Second World War the lightness of both passenger and goods traffic caused it to succumb. It closed to passengers on 7 April 1952, and goods were dealt with for a while in the unstaffed public siding until that too closed, on 6 March 1967. The station building of brick and stone still survives, although in derelict condition.

Mention must be made of the Lea as a watercress river, abounding as it does in clear pure water straight from the chalk beds. As the train crosses the viaduct over the river one can see the place where watercress beds were once worked by two brothers. This branch of husbandry is still carried on in a small way, and despite its obvious advantages over soil culture it must have been a daunting prospect to have to stand in the river carefully cropping the cress in all weathers; however, the two brothers in question are reputed to

Top
Chiltern Green station on 13 July 1939 with a 'down' express approaching headed by Jubilee class 4-6-0 5598 'Basutoland'.

Centre
Class 4F 0-6-0 4082 passing Chiltern Green with a pick-up freight on 13 July 1939.

Bottom
Luton Midland in 1907. Passengers await the arrival of an 'up' express and the stationmaster is positioned to catch sight of it as it rounds the curve to the north of the station.

have been unusually healthy.

Just beyond the viaduct on the right is a churchyard where stands the unusual Gothic tomb of Sir Julius Wernher, the financier and diamond merchant, a contemporary of Cecil Rhodes, and a pioneer in the vast Kimberley diamond-mine workings. His home was at Luton Hoo.

Luton was first served by a railway on 3 May 1858, when a line to the town was opened by the Luton, Dunstable & Welwyn Junction Railway Company, as an extension of the Welwyn & Hertford Railway, thus giving this centre of the straw plait industry its first rail outlet via the Great Northern Railway to London. A return trip to Dunstable then cost passengers mere 2½d (about 1p).

The track to Welwyn was completed in 1860 and the line was absorbed by the Great Northern the following year; it remained in use until 26 April 1965 for passenger services, and closed completely two months later.

The adjacent Midland Railway station was opened for goods traffic from 16 December 1867, the first passenger business being on 13 July 1868, providing travellers to London with an alternative and slightly quicker route. By 1887 some eight expresses and eight stopping trains were running daily to and from London. There was also a limited service to and from Bedford and Leicester, plus a further three trains each way daily on the Hemel Hempstead branch.

By 1910 Luton was expanding

Top
Luton's George Street in about 1904. The public water fountain seems to be a popular place to meet and even to lie down for a snooze.

Centre
The Midland station at Luton in about 1900, with passengers in the Victorian dress of the period; in the foreground a lady plays a barrel organ.

Bottom
Congestion in Luton Midland goods yard with a cart laden with wooden hatboxes waiting to be delivered.

rapidly and the town council was able to advertise as follows:

To Manufacturers and others seeking
Sites for Works,
LUTON, BEDFORDSHIRE
offers many attractions

Situation – *30 miles north of London.* Exceptional Railway facilities. Land in advantageous positions at moderate prices. Abundant supply of pure water at cheap rates. Cheap gas of excellent quality. Municipal electric supply; very low rate for power. Abundant houses for industrial classes at low rentals. Splendid educational facilities, elementary and secondary. Abundant well-paid occupation for female operatives
Enquiries welcomed by:
   BRUCE PENNY, Town Clerk,
    Town Hall, LUTON
   THOMAS KEENS, Secretary
    Chamber of Commerce.
(Secretaries of the Joint Committee of the Town Council and Chamber of Commerce on New Industries.)

As Luton developed so did the frequency of its train services, and the variety of goods passing through the company's yards. By 1910 there were some thirteen expresses and twenty-three local trains calling at Luton each way daily. Four of the 'up' expresses stopped only to set down as required on trains from Scotland, the North and Leicester, while one was a slip coach dropped from the express from Liverpool, Manchester, Bradford and Leeds.

   The station was an early candidate for modernization by the LMS, firstly in 1937, while in 1960 a further platform was brought into use with the introduction of diesel railcar suburban services into and out of St Pancras. Further alterations have recently been made in connection with the electrification of the main line between St Pancras and Bedford.

   When Luton station was originally

Top
A Luton straw-hat maker's workroom with girls busily working away at a variety of boaters. Note that both gas and incandescent lighting is available – no doubt the latter made winter working much easier.

Centre
The Vauxhall Motors old erecting shop at Luton, with 'A' type chassis and one with the distinctive 'Prince Henry' nose being assembled in about 1910.

Bottom
Rarely used for passenger trains, a BR Standard Class 9F 2-10-0 92153 accelerates through Luton with an 'up' relief train on 2 August 1958.

built a large public recreation area known as 'Great Moor' had to be cut through to make the line. A local philanthropist, John Crawley, provided a large open space for the public, known now as 'People's Park', while he himself bought up the remnants of the Moor and developed them.

Luton today wears a modern face, with a fine shopping precinct in the Arndale Centre. This centre, together with a huge multi-storey car park, effectively walls off and isolates the old area adjacent to the station, which now has a very poor and unimposing access from the town side. Although the town was once famous as a centre for the straw-hat trade, the changing male fashions of the early part of this century emancipated men from straw hats even more than from top hats (which continued to be the favoured gear for the bridegroom, the under-taker and the important stationmaster). Modern industry in the shape of engineering, and particularly in the production of the motor car, has largely saved the town from the more severe consequences of the decision of Tommy Atkins that having once worn a tin hat a straw one was not for him!

When the Midland Railway came to Luton in 1868 the town had a mere 18,000 inhabitants, rising to some 24,000 by 1881, and by 1911 the figure had reached 50,000. Up until the First World War the horse was an essential part of the life of the town, but the town's growth from that date onwards was related to a change to other forms of transport, coupled with the rise of engineering in the town with Skefko, the ball-bearing manufacturers; George Kent & Sons Ltd, instrument makers; Electrolux with vacuum cleaners and washing machines; Vauxhall Motors and Commercial

Top
Kentish Town shed rarely used the Stanier 2-6-2 tank locomotives for local passenger workings, usually preferring a 2-6-4 tank. 40119 rests between workings in Luton's 'up' bay on 4 July 1959.

Centre
The exterior of Leagrave station on 8 February 1970. This station has recently been restored in preparation for the new e.m.u. services.

Bottom
Leagrave station buildings and platforms on 8 February 1970, showing the architectural features of a typical London Extension station (if one can ignore the modern cycle shed).

Cars Ltd, all making their impact. Incidentally, the first car made in the town was produced by neither of the latter firms; this distinction belongs to Hayward Tyler & Co. of Crawley Green Road who built their car in 1903. Powered by a De Dion Bouton petrol engine, it unfortunately caught fire before it had undergone its road trials and was destroyed.

Between the wars some 18,000 houses were built as the town continued to grow.

Luton Airport, opened in 1938 as a grass airfield, was transformed in the 1960s, and became a centre for package-tour holiday-makers and international flights.

Modern development proceeds, as in so many places, with apparently little regard for a sense of history or cohesion. Despite (or possibly because of) the fact that since the 1930s one-third of the entire population of the county has lived in the town, few links with the past remain. Much that was beautiful and intact when the Midland first entered the town has been swept away, and the scars are there for all to see.

Leaving Luton, the line runs past an old farmhouse on the left. This is ancient Dallow Farm, one of the five manses given by King Offa to the Abbey of St Albans in 795. Later, as private property, the farm became a meeting place for Nonconformists, including the celebrated John Bunyan, who hid there for several days.

Leagrave is the next station, now looking smart and modern; the old station buildings in brick and stone have recently been carefully restored, the remainder of the station cleaned and painted and the platforms re-surfaced. It remains in use for suburban services and is soon to receive the new electric multiple units as replacement for the life-expired diesel railcars of

Top
On a pleasant May afternoon in 1957 2-6-4 tank 42685 does business at Leagrave with a 'down' local train.

Centre
Summer day at Harlington as Class 3P 4-4-0 757 heads a 'down' express through the station while a class 4F 3967 works in the goods yard.

Bottom
Harlington station and its signal box on the platform, unusually complete with advertisement hoardings on 8 February 1970.

the 1960s.

The village, named after the river which has its source close to the station, was once a simple country settlement with a population of only 800 at the end of the nineteenth century. However, since 1900 the spreading tentacles of housing developments around the village have almost linked up with the outskirts of Luton, and modern blocks of flats now rise amid the suburban housing estates around the old village centre.

The railway, from a point just south of here, has taken advantage of the work of the river which, over the centuries, has worn a deep cutting through the chalk down. The Midland line was constructed to use this valley, while further north towards Harlington is the Charlton Cutting, upwards of one mile in length, which also passes through the chalk.

A mile beyond Leagrave, 33 miles and 60 chains out of St Pancras, the route reaches the summit of the London and Bedford line before it sweeps to the right, past the Sundon Lime & Cement works and the private sidings belonging to Forders (later the London Brick Company).

A little further north the railway passes a spot where began a chain of events which resulted in one of the greatest English books ever written, for it was at a farmhouse near Harlington that John Bunyan was arrested for preaching at a conventicle, committed for trial and imprisoned in Bedford gaol. But for the trials and rigours of this experience, he might never have been granted the introspective insight which resulted in that literary jewel *Pilgrim's Progress*.

Harlington village stands on gault clay to the right of its station, once called Harlington for Toddington. However, by 1867 the latter place had lost its former importance. The liaison

Top
A detailed view of Harlington station buildings in October 1968.

Centre
Westoning village just after the turn of the century, as a cart makes its leisurely way down the main street and a couple of local residents take time off to just stand and gaze around them. Teas are available in the cottage to the left.

Bottom
High Street, Flitwick in about 1902, with ladies out for an airing in their long dresses and a group of children playing beside the fence.

between Henrietta Wentworth and the Duke of Monmouth, illegitimate son of the king, was conducted largely in and around Toddington Manor. However, Monmouth was executed after defeat at the Battle of Sedgemoor in 1685, Henrietta died the following April, and Toddington's fortunes went into slow decline as time obliterated the memories of that event in history.

The station at Harlington was opened with the line on 13 July 1868 to provide a service of stopping trains for the local community. It survives today to continue the facility and has recently been modernized; the splendid station buildings, built of stone and brick, have re-emerged from decades of soot and grime to grace the neighbourhood again with their presence.

The line next passes Westoning village on the left and comes to Flitwick station and its associated village standing on the river Ivel. Flitwick had a population of just over 1000 at the turn of the century; its old manor house stands half a mile west of the village.

The station was one of three opened on the same date, 2 May 1870, to provide local train services for the growing community in the village. It continues to serve today's residents, and the old brick and stone buildings have recently been restored to something like their original glory in anticipation of the new electric trains due to begin running in 1983.

A mile and a half further north is Ampthill, where the station is a good mile from another village steeped in history. In the church here lies the body of Richard Nicholls, first English Governor of New York, which he captured and named in honour of the Duke of York. Beneath his effigy lies the cause of his departure from this life – the cannon ball that killed him

Top
Flitwick station in about 1908 just after the departure of a 'down' train. The advertisements on the waiting room include Venus Soap and Veno's Cough Cure.

Centre
Flitwick station again (this time in about 1960) with the same waiting room still in use; 'Jubilee' class 4-6-0 45636 'Uganda' approaches with an 'up' train of coaches in the 'plum and spilt milk' livery.

Bottom
Ampthill station in rather forlorn state and under threat of closure as it appeared on 15 April 1959. It finally closed on 4 May of that year.

during the naval battle at Solebay off the Suffolk coast.

The village, of some 2500 inhabitants, busied itself with the straw-hat trade, of which the local speciality was the 'Narrow Improved' type, and also double straw plaits for dyeing, while others worked in the brewery or sweated in the local ironworks. As Ampthill had no coaching connections because it lay at the top of a steep hill, the arrival of the Midland must have considerably benefited both trade and transportation. The houses in the main street are only just pre-Victorian; Avenue House, once the home of architect Sir Albert Richardson, is the only one with a Georgian front. The village has expanded considerably in this century and now exists largely as a dormitory for inhabitants who make their living in nearby Bedford. However, they no longer travel by train, for the station, opened with the line, was closed on 4 May 1959, and intending passengers were adjured to make use of the 'excellent alternative bus service'. Now only the goods shed and yard are in use, for private commercial purposes.

A mile and a half to the north lies Ampthill New Tunnel, 718 yards long and cut beneath Ampthill Park by John Knowles, a contractor from nearby Shefford. The original old tunnel (716 yards) lies to the east, and the new tunnel was added in 1891 when the railway here was widened to four tracks.

Ampthill Park was where Lady Holland planted a great avenue of limes called 'The Alemada', at the end of which now lies the Ampthill War Memorial. Beyond the tunnel lies Ampthill House, built in 1694 by Sir John Cornwall near the ruins of a castle in which Catherine of Aragon once lodged, pending her divorce from King Henry VIII. Lacemakers in the

Top
A solitary figure is the only human in this quiet view of the Market Place at Ampthill as it was about 1906. The hotel advertises 'Good livery and bait stables. Traps on hire'.

Centre
A familiar landmark to all travellers on the Midland route are the numerous chimneys of the London Brick Company's works at Stewartby, with the model village stretched out below.

Bottom
Mechanical 'navvies' at work at the Stewartby Pit excavating clay for the millions of bricks produced here every year.

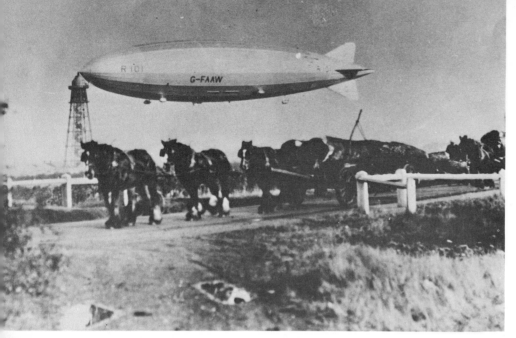

area observed St Catherine's Feast Day in her honour by drinking tea and eating special Cattern pies; the local rhyme about this runs:

Rise maids arise!
Bake your Cattern pies,
Bake enough and bake no waste,
So that the old bell-man
May have a taste!

Ampthill is in the centre of the county and from here the line runs more or less straight all the way to Bedford. On the left, piercing the skyline, stands the vast array of tall brick chimneys which marks the site of the London Brick Company's Stewartby works. Here the famous red bricks and tiles are still made, but perhaps not in so many thousands as in Midland days. Bricks have been made in these parts for centuries, but the present-day works sprang up around Wootton Pillinge, a hamlet of only two farms, where today stands a model village created in 1926 around the brickworks. It became a civil parish in 1937. Now, after decades of working, the area around is scarred by the extensive deep excavations made in order to extract the Oxford clay, while along the skyline stand the myriad sentinel chimneys of the Hoffman-type kilns used to fire the bricks.

The works are named after Halley Stewart, the co-partner of an early brick pioneer Bernard Forder who, in Queen Victoria's Diamond Jubilee year, opened works at both Elstow and Wootton Pillinge. Halley Stewart joined Forder in 1900 and this one-time junior bank clerk, with a brilliant business brain, steered the venture to great success. He was later knighted. The village was named after him in 1937, the year in which he died at the great age of ninety-nine. By this time the company was producing 700

Bunyan Cottage, Elstow.

Top
The airship R101 at her moorings at Cardington before her fateful maiden voyage on 5 October 1930, when she crashed killing 46 passengers.

Centre
The birthplace of the famous John Bunyan at Elstow, with an inquisitive group of children peering in at the window. This photograph was taken in about 1904.

Bottom
Bill Fuller and his son Fred at work with a two-horse binding machine at Elstow Knothole farm in about 1928.

million bricks a year, and eventually acquired almost complete dominance of the British brickmaking trade. Today it still continues to produce high-quality bricks for every purpose and makes notable efforts to restore exploited ground and minimize environmental damage.

The railway now runs down to the great plain of the Ouse, fourth longest river in England, and approaches Cardington to the right, with its two giant hangars and a mooring tower, sad mementoes of the romantic, but short-lived age of the great airships. Following early and mainly successful designs, the Airship Guarantee Company was given a contract to build the R100 as a commercial venture, while the Air Ministry undertook the construction of the sister ship R101. However, the dream of a passage to India, where the 100 travellers would spend 'six days amid the clouds and the stars touching only at a mooring tower at Ismailia in Egypt' was shattered on her maiden flight when she crashed at Beauvais in France on 5 October 1930 killing 46 passengers. The sister ship, R100, was scrapped the following year and the ambitious

programme was brought to an untimely end. However, some familiar dirigibles may still be seen here (used for training parachutists) reminding us of the successful Second World War application of 'lighter than air' craft.

A little further to the north and nearer the line lies the village of Elstow. Here, in 1628, was born the world-famous son of a local metalsmith – John Bunyan. The church here is the one in which Bunyan practised (later under protest it must be admitted!) the art of bell-ringing, and it was in

Top
Delightful Victorian village scene at Elstow, taken by the Midland Railway Official Photographer on 15 June 1893 for publicity purposes. The man on the left is carrying two milk churns on a yoke while the old gent on the right, possibly roadmending, appears to have a hole in his bucket!

Bottom
A village lacemaker outside her cottage, 'a stilly hamlet home that vies with an earthly paradise'.

this village that he used to dance to the fiddle and pipe. It is said that the village fair at Elstow prompted much of the material for the Vanity Fair section of his book. His later imprisonment and the writing of *Pilgrim's Progress* is a matter of record, and is referred to on page 76.

After crossing the former London & North Western Railway line from Bletchley to Cambridge (where below to the right once lay Kempston & Elstow Halt) the line runs into Bedford, where that company also had a station. Before examining this interesting town, we must relate a curious tale concerning the LNWR line just mentioned and the old Midland line to Hitchin, which once crossed each other on the level just south of Bedford. Quite early in the line's history, the driver of a North Western train proceeded over this crossing after failing to stop at the signals protecting it, and as he did so his train was struck by a Midland train running under clear signals. One passenger was killed and four were injured. When the inquiry was held it was found that both drivers were named John Perkins! This highly dangerous level crossing was eliminated in 1885 with the provision by the Midland of a flyover.

The Midland station at Bedford, on the original Hitchin line, was built upon land formerly known as 'Freemen's Common', and was completed by the end of January 1859, opening for business on 1 February. It was much altered later when work on the London Extension was being carried out in the mid to late 1860s, and yet again there were alterations to the trackwork in 1890 when the west curve, bypassing the station, was constructed to enable express trains to run past without calling. The Queen's Park road overbridge, built originally

Top
An old gentleman admiring one of Samuel Johnson's beautiful single-wheelers, in this case No. 171, at Bedford in about 1900.

Centre
One of the last compounds in service, No. 41143, on an 'up' stopping train about to depart from Bedford in 1957.

Bottom
Bedford Midland Road station in early BR days, with the original porte-cochère on the right of the picture. View taken on 8 April 1953.

to replace a dangerous level crossing, had to be further extended to suit. In recent years a brand-new Bedford station has been constructed some 200 yards to the north of the original, involving the complete remodelling of all the permanent way in the station and sidings area.

The old station with its graceful cast-iron awnings and station buildings, many of which dated back to the Leicester–Hitchin line opening, has been swept away. It was planned that the awnings should be taken down and re-erected at the Midland Railway Centre in Derbyshire, since they were in fact 'listed' by the Department of the Environment. However, when dismantling took place, the whole lot collapsed like a pack of cards and unfortunately nothing could be rescued.'

The new station, of modern design with glass walls and glass-reinforced plastic panelling, makes much use of modern materials and current artistic architectural trends; although no doubt functional and simple to maintain, it seems cold and impersonal. Modern train-describing panels are situated on each of the three main platforms, built on a new alignment adjacent to a long sweeping curve which meets the 1890 bypassing main-line twin tracks some distance beyond each end of the station. The new arrangements have enabled a new set of sidings to be built to accommodate the new Class 317 electric multiple units shortly to be introduced on to the line under the 24kV electrificaton scheme between Bedford and St Pancras, or the 'Bedpan' line as it has now become known. Of the old station only a single-bay platform at the south end and its associated buildings for newspapers and other traffic now remain.

The town of Bedford remains a pleasant, well-preserved place with

Top
A view of the Midland Extension platforms looking south from the footbridge in June 1976. Nothing now exists of the station seen here.

Centre
An Edwardian street scene is typified in this view of the High Street in Bedford about 1914. Cars are not yet in evidence but cycles abound.

Bottom
The time is just before the outbreak of the First World War as these Bedfordians enjoy an afternoon stroll beside the river Ouse.

good modern shopping facilities set beside the old buildings; it has managed to retain its character very well, compared to its near neighbour Luton. Bedford was, and is, a town of schools and churches, and its old grammar school has a notable history; but as a manufacturing centre it also made and still makes a significant contribution, chiefly in engineering.

There were many late-Victorian and Edwardian engineering firms that came to Bedford. In 1894, W. H. Allen was travelling northward on his way to the Midland headquarters town at Derby to examine potential sites for an improved works for his firm, founded in 1880. Adjacent to the station he spotted a site of some 13 acres; he looked no further, left the train and purchased the site, where he proceeded to set up his Queens Engineering Works. The Midland Railway itself once seriously considered building a locomotive, carriage and wagon works in the town following the opening of the London Extension in 1868, but the plan was never adopted.

Top left
A modern Saturday market scene in Bedford as shoppers seek bargains in the open air beneath the thoughtful statue of John Howard (1726–1790).

Bottom left
The push-and-pull train which worked the Northampton services for a number of years stands in the 'up' side bay platform at Bedford (which was the original Leciester-Hitchin 'down' platform). The engine is 2-6-2 tank 41272 and in the 1930s and 1940s Midland 0-4-4T 1272 worked the same service.

Top right
An old Kirtley 0-6-0, No. 642, heads special train of bridge girders throug Bedford on 12 October 1905. The engine carries the old MR headcode in lamps.

Centre right
Bedford station as it was in 1914 seen here looking north. At the rear of the station on the extreme left is an old Pullman car body, once one of the Midland's own day cars.

Bottom right
Johnson 4-2-2 No. 4, built at Derby in 1892, stands on Bedford shed awaiting its turn of duty. The driver's name and the home shed are painted on the side of the headlamps.

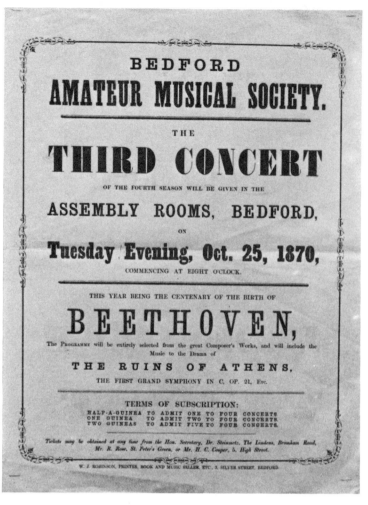

Above left
Bunyan's statue and the Church of St Peter de Merton in Bedford. The statue was presented to the town by Hastings, the 9th Duke of Bedford, on 10 June 1874.

Above right
Concert bill for the Bedford Amateur Musical Society featuring the music of Beethoven. A season ticket for five persons cost a mere two guineas!

The Ouse adds to the charm of the town centre and is an attractive asset. A tablet affixed to the new bridge of 1813 records the fact that in a jailhouse which once stood near one of the piers, John Bunyan worked at his magnum opus *Pilgrim's Progress*.

Leaving Bedford, the line is now on the track of the original Leicester to Hitchin line, of course, and between the former city and Bedford it rises to and falls from five summit levels. Two of these are on a considerable gradient: the Irchester and Desborough banks, each of which rises by some fifty feet a mile for about four miles, on a rise of 200 feet in all. The engineer for this

stretch of the line was once tackled on the subject and asked whether tunnels and viaducts might not have made for easier levels to be attained, to which he replied that the money was just not available. The chairman, John Ellis, had told engineers Charles Liddell and John Crossley, 'Here is £900,000 to make your line with. If it can't be done for that, it can't be done at all. So you must put all your fine notions in your pocket and go and do it for £15,000 a mile.' Crossley later reported that the 63 miles of line were not built without a great deal of scraping and the help of the best contractor, Thomas Brassey, to do the work.

5
Over Sharnbrook into Northamptonshire

North of Bedford, beyond Bromham Viaduct and over the Ouse, is a former junction from where the line to Northampton branched off to the left. A link between Bedford and Cambridge was proposed as early as 1845, but it was not until 1862 that the towns were joined: the Northampton line was not completed until 1872. Charles Liddell had surveyed a likely route for the latter in 1864; this proved to be almost the one finally adopted by the Bedford & Northampton Railway Company under powers granted on 5 July 1865 to construct a line joining the Midland at Oakley Unction, just north of Bedford. The Midland bought out the smaller company on 31 December 1885 and added the branch to their system.

It was originally proposed that there should be a separate terminus at Bedford. However, this plan was dropped because of extortionate demands from the owners of the land and property needed to make the line; by the alternative use of the Midland

station, some £20,000 could be saved.

The line was duly opened on 10 June 1872. Its route left the main line at Oakley Junction, crossing the main Bedford to Northampton road by means of a fine single-arched stone bridge, thence arriving at Turvey, a pleasant stone-built station standing about one mile from the village it aimed to serve. The line continued onwards via Olney and Horton and duly arrived in Northampton. Before this line opened, passengers travelling between Northampton and Bedford had a service of some four trains in each direction, but were obliged to change trains at Wellingborough and travel from there via the LNWR line. The new line had an extra train per day in each direction, but only three called at Horton (later Piddington & Horton).

The Midland's Northampton station at Bridge Street was closed on 3 July 1939, from which date the London & North Western station at Northampton (Castle) was used. The line to

Northampton was latterly worked by push-pull trains and was closed completely on 31 March 1962; the Bedford to Cambridge section survived a little longer until 1 January 1968, when it too closed.

Three miles north of Bedford stood Oakley station itself, with the village on its left. Today the village is gradually becoming merged with nearby Clapham, whose fine church, with its lofty tower soaring 85 feet into the sky, stands on the right of the line. It is one of the best examples of unbuttressed early Saxon work in the country; it dates from the tenth century and is dedicated to St Thomas à Becket.

Oakley station opened with the rest of the line on 7 May 1857, became a casualty of falling receipts a century later and was closed to passenger traffic on 15 September 1958. It retained its goods services until it was closed completely on 1 August 1963. The brick-built station building remains standing but is unused; the

goods yard is used by a local haulage firm.

It was just to the north of Oakley, before milepost 54 and on a 400-yard stretch of level track that, in 1903, the Midland laid down its first water troughs designed to enable express trains to pick up water without the need for a stop, by means of a scoop on the tender from a trough between the rails. Other troughs were later laid at Hathern, near Loughborough, near Melton Mowbray and at Blea Moor on the Settle–Carlisle line in 1907. Before that date some express locomotives had been provided with extra-large bogie tenders, nicknamed water carts, which were capable of holding 4000 gallons of water.

This particular stretch demonstrates the severity of the task of construction: in the space of a mere seven miles it crosses the Ouse no less than seven times (from a point just south of Bedford to just short of Sharnbrook station) by means of one river bridge and the Bromham, Clapham, Oakley, Milton, Radwell and Sharnbrook Viaducts. The river in the area is prone to flooding, which is why the railway was built at such an elevated level. Indeed, even some roads in the locality have elevated wooden causeways built to enable travellers on foot to negotiate the lower levels of the river valley. The Ouse itself, the fourth longest English river and some 156 miles in length, eventually flows out to sea at the southern corner of the Wash and is navigable by small craft all the way to Northampton.

Previous page
A superb action shot of 'Jubilee' class 4-6-0 45561 'Saskatchewan' as it storms up the bank with a 'down' express past the lonely Souldrop signal box on 21 April 1960.

Left
The attractive stone buildings of Turvey station on the line to Northampton on a bleak 3 March 1962.

Top right
Midland Railway notice dated 1909, as photographed on 3 March 1962 at Turvey station. The fire buckets were missing!

Centre right
Oakley station looking south as a double-headed 'down' train approaches. The leading engine is one of Johnson's 4-2-2 'spinners'. To the extreme right in the goods yard is a typical Midland coal merchant's office block with Messrs Ellis & Everard in occupation.

Bottom right
A close-up view of the station buildings at Oakley in BR days.

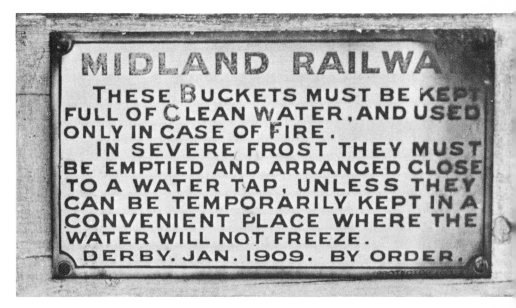

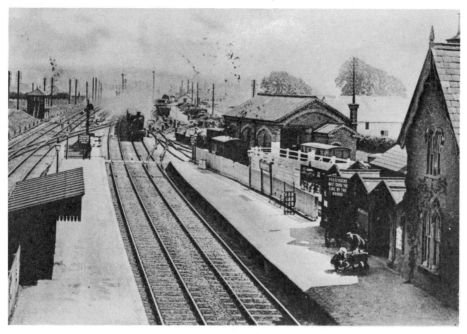

The railway now begins a long steep climb on a gradient of 1 in 119 to Sharnbrook Summit. Part of the route includes the site of Sharnbrook station, once serving the nearby village which, together with Colworth Farm, had a population of some 680 at the turn of the century. The station, opened with the line, was closed on 2 May 1960 and the station building itself is no longer standing; however, the goods yard buildings are still intact and are used for private business purposes. At the time of closure, intending passengers were encouraged to patronize the United Counties Omnibus Co. Ltd or the local firm of Birch Brothers Ltd. Parcels and pasenger-train merchandise were to be dealt with at Wellingborough, and any local passengers intrepid enough to consider a rail journey, despite the difficulty of starting it, were advised to go to Bedford!

This part of north-west Bedfordshire is known as 'stone-country', since stone is the predominant building material.

It is at Sharnbrook, with its stone and brick houses, that the only school catering for 13–18-year-olds exists to serve the whole area, and consequently the village sees a daily stream of children from neighbouring areas travelling in by bus and car for their daily dose of modern education, rather than as in former times by the (surely more satisfying) steam train.

As the line climbs steeply towards the summit it passes the site of lonely Souldrop signal box and away to the right is Souldrop church (a corruption

Top
Busy Sharnbrook station looking south with a local train approaching. A passenger on the platform receives help with his luggage from a friendly porter.

Centre
Sharnbrook village main street with no pavements, as it was about 1905.

Bottom
Stoke corn mill near Sharnbrook, mentioned in the Domesday Book, was one of more than a hundred such water mills scattered throughout Bedfordshire:

Back of the Bread is the Flour,
And back of the Flour is the Mill.
Back of the Mill is the Sun and the Shower
And the Wind and the Father's Will.

of Soulthorp) with its lovely thirteenth-century brooch spire. From the train one can look clear through the spire by means of the two tiers of windows set within it. This church once belonged to the Knights Hospitaller.

As the line nears Sharnbrook Summit, 340 feet above sea level, and then runs down the other side, it can be observed at this point that the two goods lines on the right have parted company with the two passenger lines and run through Sharnbrook Tunnel, 1860 yards long. The widening here and the construction of the tunnel was carried out in the early 1880s in order to quadruple the line, thereby making it possible to separate the growing volume of goods and mineral traffic from passenger traffic. The former line now takes the 3½-mile-long Wymington Deviation, near Wymington village, with its easier ruling gradient of 1 in 200. This diversionary route was opened for traffic on 4 May 1884.

In steam days the original Sharnbrook bank was always a major obstacle to be surmounted, and on many occasions took its toll of trains travelling in both directions because of the severe gradients. This happened especially to the more slowly moving and heavily loaded freight trains, and particularly in autumn and winter when there were fallen leaves, ice and snow to contend with. Today's trains, hauled by diesel locomotives, seem to give the climb scant respect as they sweep easily up the grade and over the summit, hardly faltering in pace.

Top
A view of Sharnbrook station from the south as it was on 13 April 1959. The station closed on 2 May 1950 and only the goods yard buildings remain.

Centre
A last defiant fling by a compound on an express passenger train, as 41173 of Trafford Park shed gallops up the grade with a ten-coach relief through Sharnbrook station on 16 August 1958.

Bottom
43929 with an 'up' local goods stands by the goods shed at Sharnbrook; 43977 passes on the 'up' goods line with a special empty stock on 16 August 1958.

The goods lines lie below the tunnel mound to the right of the passenger lines, surmounted at intervals by the brick-built ventilating shafts, and thus avoiding the worst part of the climb by passing *through* the summit rather than over it.

The route now goes on over a tributary of the Nene and into Northamptonshire, where the first station is at Irchester, 62¾ miles from London. Irchester, with its church and village to the left of the line, has been described as an overgrown village. As its name suggests, the place has Roman connections. A little to the north of the station, where the railway crosses the valley of the Nene, there was once a Roman fort. Some remains, including 400 skeletons, were discovered in 1874 together with two stone coffins; while in the grounds of the nearby Tudor-style Chester House, massive Corinthian capitals and column bases have been uncovered. Many of the Irchester population (some 2300 at the turn of the century) were engaged in shoemaking, while the nearby ironstone workings employed others; for this is the area of ironstone, one of the major items of mineral traffic carried by the Midland and its successors over the years. Some of the ironstone, which is both rich and easily fusible, was smelted in works locally, but the bulk was transported by rail into Yorkshire, Derbyshire and North Wales. It was found more profitable, with the possibility of bulk transport by rail, to take the ore to where the coal was rather than vice versa.

Irchester, unique in that the station building sat astride the line on the road overbridge, was closed on 7 March 1960 to passenger traffic and for goods on 4 January 1965. Leaving Irchester on the right is the formation of the former Midland branch from Wellingborough to Higham Ferrers,

Top
The ornate station at Irchester, unique on this line in being built on the overbridge, unlike any other intermediate station. View taken on 13 April 1959.

Centre
Irchester station on 20 May 1953 as a Stanier Class 8F hauls an 'up' freight southwards.

Bottom
A double-headed train about to leave Higham Ferrers, possibly on the opening day, behind tanks 0-4-4 No. 2022 and 0-6-0 No. 212. The branch from Wellingborough opened on 1 May 1894.

some 5¼ miles distant, with an intermediate station at Rushden, opened for goods traffic on 1 September 1893 and for passengers on 1 May 1894. The latter village is the more commercial of the two places, notable as the home of the John White footwear firm, celebrated for supplying boots and shoes to the armed forces. Higham still retains an air of respectability, cleanliness and Nonconformism. Its most distinguished son was Henry Chichele, Archbishop of Canterbury, who died in 1443; the remains of his college can be seen in College Street.

In its heyday the branch boasted a dozen or so weekday trains with a couple of extra ones on Saturdays. In Midland days tank engines and the occasional 2-4-0 and 0-6-0 tender

Top
The cavernous excavation of Stewart & Lloyd's ironstone pits at Irchester complete with its own mineral lines and train.

Bottom left
A distant view of Irchester station clearly showing its location on the overbridge.

Bottom right
Farndish Road, Irchester with its solidly built palisaded villas providing a good standard of housing for the local community in the latter part of the nineteenth century.

FARNDISH ROAD, IRCHESTER

engine provided the motive power. The Wellingborough shed was not above commandeering 2-6-2 tank locomotives on their way back to Kentish Town after repair at Derby, and keeping them for a couple of days or so to work the branch traffic! Later on, still stranger locomotives were used, including ex-L & Y 2-4-2T 50650. The branch closed for passenger traffic on 15 June 1959 and completely for all traffic on 3 February 1969.

Wellingborough is reached via the valley of the Nene (another river flowing into the Wash) by means of a magnificent four-arch viaduct, and as it approaches the town the line crosses over the formation of the former London & North Western Railway from Northampton and Peterborough, of which little trace now remains. It then arrives at the place where the former branch from the left brought the Midland's own connecting line from the LNWR station into its own. The LNWR opened their station on 1 October 1866 at London Road, but the major services for Wellingborough were always those provided by the Midland, and trains to London amounted to only a dozen or so on weekdays.

The main station at Wellingborough has old buildings designed by C. A. Driver which have been much altered over the years. Yet the station still retains a Midland 'feel' and, in fact, is one of those which still bear the marks of the steam age; with its well weathered brickwork and grimy, sooted and yellowing glass canopy, it is much the worse for wear and in need of repair, as was the old footbridge, which was closed early in 1983 for safety reasons.

Wellingborough was also the site of a large locomotive depot and extensive associated sidings; it was situated some 65 miles from St Pancras which made it a convenient day's work for a goods locomotive. The first roundhouse

Top
Compound 4-4-0 No. 1104 entering Wellingborough from the north with a heavy train of thirteen bogie coaches on 25 May 1931.

Centre
A modern view of the old Wellingborough station buildings still retaining some of the original canopy, albeit in need of repair.

Bottom
Class 5 4-6-0 No. 45279 of Kentish Town depot runs into Wellingborough in March 1958 with an 'up' parcels train. These locomotives were real maids of all work.

for locomotives dated from 1868 and the second from 1872. Freight and mineral traffic was worked by the locomotives from here; in LMS days these included the huge Beyer Garratt 2-6-6-2 locomotives, the firing of which has been the downfall of many a trainee fireman. Passenger turns included the local services to Bedford, Leicester and Kettering as well as the Higham Ferrers branch mentioned before. No. 1 shed was demolished in July 1964, while a private contractor now uses No. 2 shed.

Wellingborough itself, to the left of the line, is a market town which rapidly grew from 5000 inhabitants in 1851 until, in the late 1880s, some 14,000 people lived there, engaged in the manufacture of boots and shoes (sent largely via the Midland to the London markets) and in the smelting of iron ore. The town derives its name from the wells or springs, whose alleged curative powers were sufficiently strong to persuade King Charles I and his queen to stay under canvas in the town for nine days in order to partake of the waters.

Wellingborough was largely destroyed by a disastrous fire in 1738, and a fair proportion of the rebuilt town still remains, along with a few older buildings that somehow escaped the inferno. Mechanization of the shoe trade later attracted agricultural workers into the town to improve their lot, and today some 85,000 people live and work here.

Notable buildings include Wellingborough's public school; the remains of Croyland Abbey with its connections with Alfred the Good; and St Mary's church, begun in 1908 and completed in 1975 – said to be Sir Ninian Comper's favourite building. All Hallows church boasts some fine windows by John Piper.

Top
A fine study of Wellingborough looking south as Royal Scot class loco 46152 'The King's Dragoon Guardsman' runs through the station with a St Pancras–Manchester express on 23 May 1958.

Centre
A view of part of the wreckage in the Wellingborough accident on 2 September 1898, caused when a platform trolley ran off into the path of the Manchester express. The crew and six passengers were killed and sixty-five injured.

Bottom
The Higham Ferrers branch train headed by Midland 0-4-4 tank No. 58091 at Wellingborough on 18 April 1951.

The line runs on through country rich in ironstone, and the next stop is Finedon station built, like so many others, some distance from the village; which in this case cannot even be seen from the line. This two-platform station, one of the island type, was served by local passenger trains. Just south of the station were the quite extensive mineral sidings which provided the outlet for the Excelsior stone works in addition to the Finedon Hill mines which were linked by a tramway to an elevated tipping dock. This was worked at one time by horses, but in 1880 the form of traction changed to an endless rope worked by a stationary steam engine, with a steam hoist to raise the tubs for tipping into the standard-gauge wagons at the dock. In later years steam locomotives were introduced to work the line.

Always inconvenient, and becoming increasingly so in the motorized twentieth century, the station succumbed to the times and closed for passenger traffic on 2 December 1940 and for all traffic from 6 July 1964.

The village, a mile and a half to the south-east, housed 4129 inhabitants in 1900; many of the males were employed in the various ironstone pits in the neighbourhood. Just beyond the village lies the round church-like Volta Tower, erected by a sorrowing local squire as a memorial to his son who was lost in the wreck of the ship *Volta* in 1863. The building now serves as a farm.

A short distance to the north lay the next station, Isham and Burton Latimer, built and opened with the line to serve these two neighbouring villages to the south and to the east of

Top
The 'down' motor train from Northampton passing Finedon station signal box on 10 March 1963 headed by BR Standard 2-6-2 tank 84005.

Centre
Isham and Burton Latimer station looking north with the goods lines and associated sidings to the right. Note the popular advertisements for Pears Soap and Epps's Cocoa.

Bottom
A view of the main street at Burton Latimer in about 1910, which evokes memories of that period so well. The Duke's Arms on the right, where Phipps' Ales and Stouts are on tap, also provides accommodation for cyclists, and perhaps the young man in the left foreground (properly clad in full cycling gear) is a guest. The usual group of curious children, some with cycles, looks on.

the station respectively. The station, which stood on the pleasant country lane joining the villages, survived until 2 November 1950, when it closed. The brick-built station building, to the west of the 'down' line, still stands, now lonely and forlorn in its sylvan setting.

Isham takes its name from the Isham family. Robert was the attorney of King Edward IV's sister, and his wife, Elizabeth Woodville, was of Northampton stock. Its neighbouring village, Burton Latimer, lies nearer to the outskirts of Kettering, and the Midland once served the ironstone mine and a flour mill with sidings here, while today's industry includes the large Weetabix cereal factory. The village, with a pleasant high street, manages to retain some of its former charm, but proximity to the larger town threatens the continuance of that happy state.

Remains of another branch line now lie to the right of the main line – the Midland branch which ran to Thrapston, thence to Huntingdon, where it had a station, and on to Cambridge (by courtesy of running powers), where the Midland had its own goods station and small loco shed. This line was originally part of the South Midland Railway Scheme of 1846, but was not actually built until the Kettering, Thrapston & Huntingdon Railway Company obtained an Act in 1862 to build the 26-mile connection between the Midland at Kettering and the Great Eastern at Huntingdon. Yet again, the Midland agreed to work the new line, which was opened for goods traffic on 21 February and for passenger trains from 1 March 1866. The line became vested in the Midland on 6 August 1897 and was always rural by nature, with only half a dozen or so leisurely-paced stopping trains daily. Passenger traffic ceased on 15 June 1959.

Just before Kettering another

Top
Ex-LNER and formerly Great Eastern Railway Class J15 0-6-0 65457 leaves Kettering with the 5.25 p.m. train for Cambridge on 18 July 1958, taking along for good measure of couple of loaded cattle wagons.

Centre
A sunny Sunday afternoon and LMS 2-6-0 'Crab' 42771 heads a milk train near Kettering.

Bottom
Former Midland compound 4-4-0 1006 stands at Kettering with a 'down' train which includes two ex-Midland clerestory carriages on 3 September 1933.

former branch joined the main line from the left. This served the Cransley and Loddington branches, and the iron and ironstone works which they linked. The Cransley branch opened on 19 February 1877, the year in which the Cransley Iron Company's blast furnaces were lit. As the ore became exhausted the Loddington branch to new deposits was opened in April 1891, providing the Midland with much traffic as a result. The Cransley Company in BR days had a part in breaking up both steam and diesel locomotives.

Kettering is fortunate in retaining one of the best and most original-looking Midland-style stations on the whole line. Its elegant cast-iron awnings of ridge-and-furrow style are almost complete, though today they are covered with modern roofing sheets. With four platforms, the station is large compared to its neighbours – as one would expect for a town of its importance. It was extensively rebuilt between 1879 and 1884 to facilitate the quadrupling of the main line and was largely rebuilt yet again in 1896. One of the features which endear it to the traveller must be its somwhat curious refreshment room (housed in the main station building) which also serves as a newspaper shop and bookstall – tea and toasties with *The Times*!

Services from Kettering ran not only north and south on the main line but also via a branch commencing at Glendon South Junction, through Manton and Melton Mowbray to Nottingham, and also to Cambridge via Thrapston and Huntingdon. There was once a through service to Cambridge from Derby and beyond using this latter route, and in BR days there was a summer Saturday through service from Leicester to Clacton-on-Sea.

The town of Kettering lies to the

Top
Now preserved Royal Scot class 4-6-0 No. 46115 'Scots Guardsman' entering Kettering on 29 March 1962 with a train from Manchester (Piccadilly) to London (St Pancras).

Centre
A modern view of Kettering station as viewed from the approach road; its condition has altered little since the end of the last century.

Bottom
Kettering station has fortunately managed to retain its fine cast-iron canopies, as this view clearly shows, though these days they are covered in modern sheeting materials.

east of the station surmounted by the crocketed spire of the church of SS Peter and Paul, dating from 1225. Called 'Kateringes' in Henry II's time, it is of Saxon origin and eventually passed into the hands of the monks of Peterborough. The traditional market, with canvas-covered stalls, is still held in the shadow of the church, on the market square beside the Corn Exchange (opened in 1862). High Street and Gold Street now embrace a pedestrian shopping precinct, while many of the town's older buildings were demolished under improvement schemes around the turn of the century and in the 1920s. The centre of Kettering seems to be undergoing a common type of metamorphosis in order to fit it somehow for the twenty-first century. Few towns manage to achieve this transition satisfactorily, and one writer has observed that Kettering appears to be in 'civic menopause'. In 1881 it had a population of 11,095, principally engaged in the manufacture of boots and shoes, currying and leather-dressing, and the manufacture of brushes and clothing of all kinds; the nearby iron-ore furnaces and the surrounding agricultural land provided employment for many more. Over the years the Midland has had a part in, and added to, the town's prosperity and even today the station has a businesslike air about it.

Kettering can boast of being the birthplace of British Christian missions, for it was in a private house towards the northern end of the town that the first English missionary meeting took place. William Carey, Andrew Fuller and a few other ministers of the Baptist Connexion, with a collection of £13 2s 6d, began the organization from which sprang one of our great Victorian missionary movements.

Top
The Market Place, Kettering in about 1904 with the traditional canvas-covered stalls selling virtually everything. The market, little changed today (except for the prices, of course) still flourishes on the same spot.

Centre
The Midland train for Cambridge at Kettering in the care of a fine old veteran Kirtley outside-framed 2-4-0 No. 20012 built at Derby in 1867. The photograph was taken on 3 July 1937.

Bottom
'Our good old annual' reads the caption as the group prepares to set off for a day's outing from the Cardigan Arms at Brigstock near Kettering.

89

We must not leave Kettering without mentioning the philanthropist Charles Wicksteed and his generous provision of Wicksteed Park, a vast open recreational area given to the town for the pleasure of inhabitants and visitors alike. Since its opening the Park has been an attraction for countless visitors, with its many amenities, including attractive flower beds and borders, lawns, a boating lake and children's playground. Wicksteed himself was a manufacturer of amusements, fairground rides and children's park playgrounds.

Kettering's near neighbour is Corby, once renowned for its extensive iron and steel works, which have now unfortunately been closed although there are plans for a vast pleasure park in the area. The works generated a lot of traffic for the Midland and its successors over the years and its closure was yet another blow to BR freight business.

Most engaging of ancient customs was the Corby Pole Fair, held every twenty years on Whit Monday, supposedly to celebrate a charter granted by Elizabeth I in 1585, freeing Corby men from various tolls and jury duties. The fair opened with the reading of the charter by the rector and the chairman of the parish council seated on a pole. Before the fair every road and lane leading into the village was closed off by strong wooden gates and everyone wishing to enter was asked to pay a toll. If men refused, they were hoisted on poles, carried to the centre of the village and locked in one of three sets of stocks until they agreed to pay. Women shared the same fate, except that they were carried to the stocks in a chair.

After leaving Kettering the line passes through pleasant undulating countryside notable for its red soil, a reminder of the riches of the ores below. It was a railway passenger travelling down this very route on one of the first trains to use the new line who made a note of the iron ore, which showed clearly in the newly made cuttings; he exploited his

Top
Public benefactor Charles Wicksteed enjoys a chat at a gala day in the park near Kettering which is named after him and which he gave to the people of the town.

Bottom
Queer goings-on at Corby Pole Fair. The gent on the pole, having refused to pay the toll demanded, has been carried into the village in this uncomfortable manner and will shortly join the others in the stocks.

observation, which resulted in the iron ore trade being commercially 'rediscovered'.

The line now arrives at Glendon Junction, from where the Kettering and Manton branch (opened for goods and mineral traffic on 1 November 1879) diverges to the right to Manton on the Syston to Peterborough line. Built primarily to open up access to the rich mineral ore deposits in this part of the country, this branch also formed a new alternative route to Nottingham, and was opened to passenger traffic on 2 February 1880.

Glendon and Rushton, which was closed on 4 January 1960 but which once served these two villages, is the next station on the route. It was originally called Rushton, and the village of that name with its tower stands on the left. Beyond the village stands Rushton Hall, once the home of the Tresham family; Sir John Tresham (whose alabaster effigy lies in the church) was the last Grand Prior of the Knights Hospitaller of England. Rushton Hall is said to have been the scene of 'unholy conclaves' of the Gunpowder Plotters in the reign of James I, and for his share in the conspiracy Sir Francis Tresham was thrown into the Tower, where he mercifully died a natural death. His head was struck from his body and preserved; it was used to decorate one of the Northampton town gates, while his possessions were seized and passed to the Lords Cullen.

The house itself dates from 1595, with many additions and rebuildings over the long years; it is now used by the Royal National Institute for the Blind as a children's school. The most intriguing building in Rushton Park is the Triangular Lodge, of which a good view is obtained to the left of the line a little distance to the north of the station. Glendon, with a population of only 57 at the turn of the century as

Top
Desborough High Street just before the First World War. Lee's shop on the right is selling boots for 1s 11d and jackets from 3s 11d. Not a sign of a motor car, as a solitary cart moves leisurely down the street.

Centre
The Market Square at Rothwell, with the fine Market House of Sir Thomas Tresham, which dates from about 1587. The Holy Trinity church stands behind it to the left.

Bottom
The station house of the former Desborough and Rothwell station, now converted into an excellent private dwelling.

Rothwell, Kettering.

91

opposed to Rushton's 503, also had a country seat nearby – Glendon Hall.

Desborough and Rothwell is the next station, finally closed on 1 January 1968. The line actually passes through the edge of Desborough, which is to the left and was notable in earlier times for the manufacture of boots, shoes and stays. Here once lived the eminent lawyer Ferdinando Pulton who compiled the Statutes of England from Magna Carta to the sixteenth year of the reign of James I. Areas of new housing now sprawl untidily around the old village heart. Desborough had a population of some 3573 at the turn of the century while neighbouring Rothwell (pronounced Rowell) boasted some 4193. This village, which lies a mile and a half to the south, is steeped in history, having an ancient Augustinian nunnery, founded by the Clare family, and a magnificent Holy Trinity church. The church is the longest parish church in the county and was built from the rich tawny local ironstone – the effect of this when one enters the church is like a burst of glory. The village today is a mixture of light industry and commerce and yet it preserves the old, for example Sir Thomas Tresham's fine

Market House, built in about 1587 as a meeting house or council house but now in a somewhat parlous state.

On the south side of the square lies the Jesus Hospital founded in 1591 by Owen Ragdale. The remainder of the now straggling village is unpretentious, but it comes alive once a year for Charter Fair week which dates back to 1204 and commences at 6 a.m. on the day after Trinity Sunday with the reading of the Charter to the local populace.

Just beyond the station, on the left, once lay a 28-chain branch serving the unlikely-sounding Desborough Co-operative Society Iron Mine, which was opened in 1906. Leaving the station behind, the line heads north-wards again past the site of historic Braybrook Castle, blown up by accident in the time of Henry IV. Later, when it was rebuilt, it received James II as a guest, but trenches and mounds are all that now remain.

The line now reaches Desboro' Summit and begins the long descent of over four miles at a gradient of 1 in 132 down the bank. Steam trains travelled very slowly when climbing this section and on one particular journey, after signals had been dismissed as the reason for little progress being made, a wise regular traveller remarked 'No, we're going slowly because of the Crimean War', and after the laughter had subsided he went on to explain the paradox and how, when the Midland projected the line, the war with Russia was at its height, money was dear and men were difficult to get. These limitations, as elsewhere on the 60-mile stretch of line, meant much shallower cuttings and much lower embankments had to be included in the engineering works, with the penalty of severe gradients. In Midland days successive generations of locomotives toiled up one side or the other of the Desborough Bank; a number of them grinding to a halt, having run short of steam in the attempt.

The line now crosses the river Welland into Leicestershire.

Top
Sir Thomas Tresham's Triangular Lodge at Rushton, symbolic of the Holy Trinity, with three sides and three of almost everything else, dates from 1597. Each side is exactly 33 feet long.

Bottom
Desborough and Rothwell station on 25 September 1906 looking south as a freight train approaches hauled by a Kirtley 0-6-0 tender locomotive.

6
Market Harborough to Leicester

Entering the southern boundary of Leicestershire, the line soon reaches Market Harborough some 83 miles from St Pancras. This is an ancient town, once spelt 'Haverburgh', which still retains much of its old charm and, although the modern age has left its mark on the centre and changed much of its surrounding area, many of the old buildings still stand. The church beside the market square is dedicated to St Dionysius, most famous perhaps for working out the dates of the Christian era to which (although quite wrong!) we are still working today. The decorated tower, surmounted by a tall and elegantly proportioned brooch spire, has been described by Nicholas Pevsner as 'one of the finest in England'. Beside the church stands the old Grammar School founded by Robert Smythe in 1614; the upper floor was at that time used as the school, while the open space below was used as a butter market.

The town's trades have included corsets, liberty bodices, hosiery,

Previous page
The 11 a.m. Leeds to London (St Pancras) approaching Market Harborough double-headed by a Kirtley 2-4-0 and Johnson 4-2-2 No. 172 in 1900.

Below
Midland compound 4-4-0 No. 1010 leaves Market Harborough with an 'up' express for St Pancras in about 1946.

rubber, agricultural machinery, boots, shoes, soups, malthouses and the growing of mushrooms, while the supply of meat from the pastures of the county via the market is also considerable. The Fernie Hunt, with kennels at nearby Great Bowden, hunts the land and provides one of the country sights for which Leicestershire is so famous.

Outside the town, on the site of one of the Second World War bomber airfields, now stands Gartree Prison, accommodating some 300 medium-term inmates.

Immediately to the left of the station stands a burial ground with a mortuary chapel which occupies the site of the old parish church of St Mary in Arden, or 'the church in the wood'. It acquired a bad reputation for the celebration of clandestine marriages which, coupled with the 'ignorant and disorderly nature of its curates', caused its privileges to be transferred to the town church. Subsequently the steeple fell into the church and left it in ruins (said by some to be God's judgement!), and today only the small chapel remains.

In 1786 a gardener called Hubbard left a guinea a year for the town church choir to sing an Easter hymn over his grave on Easter Eve, and this was still done well into the twentieth century, although the place was disused and the choir had to hurry

through the overgrown graveyard to sing by the old gardener's weed-covered mound.

The first station in Market Harborough belonged to the London and North Western Railway which began with services between Rugby and Stamford in 1850, thus providing a through service from London (Euston), the line later extending to Peterborough. This original station was approached from the Great Bowden Road, and was used by the Midland when it began services on its new Leicester and Hitchin line on 8 May 1857. The fare to King's Cross was then 7s 10d (39p) second class!

Services over the Northampton line of the LNWR began in 1859 and later still (1883) there were services over the LNWR and Great Northern Railway Joint line, which branched off the Peterborough line at Welham Junction and ran via Melton Mowbray to Saxondale Junction where it joined the GNR line to Nottingham, and at Bottesford North Junction where it joined the Great Northern line to Newark.

The Midland line joined the LNW just north of Market Harborough and originally used the latter company's metals as far as the station, where its own line branched off to the south. However, with the upsurge of traffic on the Midland line, the company decided to be a tenant no longer. It

could have constructed a completely
new route deviating to the north,
thereby leaving Market Harborough
with stations at opposite ends of the
town. Happily for future travellers, it
chose to raise the level of its own line
on a new alignment up and over the
LNWR line as it approached the town
from the east, and then to carry a new
line parallel with the LNWR lines for a
distance of 66 chains to the site of a
new joint station to be constructed in
the fork of the Midland and LNW
lines further to the south. The quadrupling of the lines through the old
station was completed in 1879, and the
Midland continued to use it until the
new station, built in LNWR style, was
opened on 14 September 1885. The
two sides of the station, serving
respectively the LNW platform to the
west and the Midland with platforms
swinging away to the south-east, were
identical, except that at first the
Midland provided an additional set of
stairs to their platform. The original
station was closed on 27 June 1885,
although there must have been a
change-over period, and presumably
the new platforms were already in use,
but the station buildings themselves
were apparently not completed until
the September.

Midland line services to London
became much improved once St
Pancras had been opened: some
fourteen trains called at Market
Harborough in each direction on
weekdays, although the fastest
expresses did not stop and passengers
were required to make their way north
to Leicester or south to Kettering by a
stopping train to make a connection
with these. St Pancras now lay, at
just over two hours' travelling time
away.

Top
The old grammar school at Market
Harborough dates back to 1614; the upper
floors were being used by the school while
the open space below was a butter market.

Centre
Market Harborough town centre with a
sheep market in full swing in about 1903.

Bottom
The London & North Western station at
Market Harborough in about 1860 and a
Rugby train ready for departure with 2-2-2
No. 35.

Market Harborough was the scene of a serious accident on 28 August 1862. The front portion of an excursion train with 250 passengers, which had left King's Cross at 7.30 p.m. bound for Burton-on-Trent, stopped at the station to take water and was run into from the rear by the second portion, carrying 240 passengers, which had left King's Cross barely five minutes later bound for Leicester. Two carriages and a van were wrecked, one passenger was killed and twenty-nine seriously injured. A special train, with four doctors on board, was despatched from Leicester and arrived on the scene within thirty minutes. The coroner's jury found the driver of the second train guilty of culpable negligence and the Midland Company was highly censured for providing insufficient braking power.

The line from Harborough to Northampton lost many of its regular services in January 1960 and finally, on 4 June 1966 (the last day of normal services), the line was thronged with enthusiasts and 'mourners' who travelled the line between Rugby and Peterborough all day. The final train, the 20.53 Rugby to Peterborough, was hauled by diesel-electric locomotive

D 5036 which travelled the line sporting
suitable wreaths and a last-train
'banner', waved away from
Harborough at 21.34½ precisely by
the booking clerk, Mr R. Baker.
Thus the people of the Welland valley
lost their only railway and the Midland
line its century-long rival and
competitor.

Harborough today hosts the new
High Speed trains of the 1980s as they
speed on their journeys, first over and
then past the now forlorn branch
formation that was once an important
cross-country route for the area.

The station itself had a face-lift in
the 1960s at a cost of £12,000 and
within the last few years some £84,000
has been spent rebuilding it. The old
buildings on the platforms have been
swept away and the station now sports
a modern canopy and a satisfactory, if
somewhat spartan, passenger amenity
block on the 'down' platform. The
station building itself fortunately
survived and was given a complete
face-lift. At its reopening in the
summer of 1981, Sir Hugh Casson
observed that the exercise had been 'a
success of conservation'.

Top left
Children in their Sunday best line up with
a brass band outside Market Harborough
station in about 1910, possibly for a
Sunday School treat.

Centre left
The famous Three Swans family hotel and
posting house at Market Harborough in
about 1909. It remains much the same
today but with a less ornate sign.

Bottom right
Fellmongers at work in Market
Harborough in the late 1860s. This
occupation caused a disturbing odour,
which did not endear it to local
inhabitants.

Top right
The old London & North Western station
at Market Harborough which was used by
the Midland until 14 September 1885 when
the new joint station was opened.

Centre right
Jubilee class 4-6-0 45618 'New Hebrides'
stands at Market Harborough with a train
for St Pancras in about 1954.

Bottom right
Market Harborough station buildings as
recently restored by British Railways,
displaying many typical features of
LNWR design.

Admittedly the coming of the railways to Harborough changed long-distance travel for many people from an infrequent and hazardous event into an everyday and reasonably comfortable experience. Before the introduction of the iron horse on rails, a traveller from Berlin wrote that he would remember for the rest of his life a journey from Leicester to Northampton undertaken in 1782. Travelling on top of a stagecoach, he recorded: 'The getting up alone was at the risk of one's life. The moment we set off I fancied I saw certain death await me. Every moment we seemed to fly into the air, so that it was almost a miracle that we still stuck to the coach and did not fall off.' By the time the coach reached Market Harborough he was almost a nervous wreck.

Beyond Market Harborough the line runs through some of the rich pasture land from which still comes prime beef, mutton and lamb. It passes over the former LNWR Rugby to Stamford single-line branch (as before described) which it left at Great Bowden Junction, and followed the Welland Valley in its meandering. The route continues onwards to the next station at East Langton – again alas now no more than a memory. Originally called simply Langton, it was renamed on 1 May 1891 and was closed on 1 January 1968. This once proud and neat little station served no fewer than five Langtons, namely East, West, Church, Thorpe and Tur Langton. These were all named after Bishop Walter de Langton, a man of strong character and wise purposes who was a friend and counsellor of Edward I and one-time Bishop of Lichfield. He himself was born at West Langton.

Another notable resident was William Hanbury, rector of Church Langton, for whom a lovely Adam-style rectory was built, and who

Top
No. 1033 accelerates past Little Bowden signal box about 1946 with signalman Reg Vines looking on.

Centre
The church at Church Langton where William Hanbury arranged for a performance of Handel's *Messiah* shortly after it was written.

Bottom
Kibworth station with the staff specially posed for the photographer (between trains, of course). The station is actually in Kibworth Beauchamp.

espoused the causes of music, philanthropy, and gardening. He laid out immense nurseries, reared young plants and trees and sent catalogues country-wide. The money thus gained was put aside to realize his one ideal, which was the founding of a third university at Church Langton to rival both the grandeur and the scholastic endeavours and achievements of Oxford and Cambridge. He then began a series of music festivals at the church, inaugurating them with Handel's *Messiah*, which was given there on 27 September 1759 – its first performance in a church, only shortly after it had been written. Two thousand people came, and the countryside was solid with carriages and carts of every kind. In 1777 Hanbury began laying out sites for the enlarged church and the university buildings but he died the following year and, although a large sum was left in trust, the trustees set aside his plan for accumulating 100 years of compound interest before commencing building; the money was spent on a variety of small schemes year by year, and the trust became merely a local charity. The local schools, originally founded in 1767 by Hanbury, had fine new premises provided out of the Trust Funds in 1873.

Next on the line is Kibworth, where lies a red-brick grammar school founded by Warwick the Kingmaker; more associations with him are connected with a field by the railway, colourfully called 'Hell's Half Acre'. The village lies to the left of the station, while the church is on the right. Nearby are the villages of Kibworth Beauchamp and Kibworth Harcourt. Kibworth was an outpost of the Leicester stocking manufacturing trade and here were two hosiery factories.

Top
Station Street at Kibworth in about 1913 with a number of folk out for a stroll. The station lies to the right beyond the row of houses.

Centre
A typical group of Midland Railway coal merchants' offices in the goods yard at Kibworth.

Bottom
Compound 4-4-0 No. 41059 near Kibworth North signalbox with a semi-fast to Leicester on 7 June 1954.

Kibworth was the scene of an unusual accident when the night Scotch Pullman train, hauled by Kirtley 2-4-0 809, stopped in a tunnel with the engine's gear in reverse on a foggy night of 9 October 1880. The driver opened the regulator to restart the train and was unaware that it was travelling backwards! He ran in this fashion for some distance before colliding with a following freight train. Two people lost their lives, and as a result of the incident the vertical reversing screw on that particular class of engine was changed to the normal type to prevent a recurrence.

The station, along with that at East Langton, closed on 1 January 1968.

On the way north this line runs past the Leicester branch of the Grand Union Canal (formerly the Leicestershire & Northants Union Canal), reminding us that when this great waterway was planned Parliament was seriously urged that if a canal was built at all it should pass no closer to a town than four miles so that local goods carriers might still make a decent living. Events during the actual building of the canal probably bore out this view, for a mob caused disturbances in Kibworth village, while some three hundred angry navvies, actually employed to dig the canal or 'cut', marched upon Leicester during a wage dispute.

Crossing a tributary of the Soar, the line now reaches the site of Great Glen station (formerly Glen Magna, and in the 1880s merely Glen) which closed to traffic on 18 June 1951 and became an unstaffed depot for goods on 27 August 1962. It finally closed completely on 6 July 1964, although the station house is still in use for private commercial purposes. The village a mile away to the right, along with neighbouring Burton Overy, was the scene of a witch hunt in 1760 when various women were ducked in a witching-stool in the idiotic belief that those who sank beneath the water were innocent while a real witch would float; innocent suspects suffered and sometimes died as well as the 'guilty'. Two other local women were made to stand in the pillory on this occasion for false accusations. Thus superstition and ignorance survived in the country villages. It was said of

Great Glen at the time that it was 'great for nothing except containing more dogs than honest men'.

Two miles north of Great Glen the line crosses the Leicester–Northampton road, passes the unusual signal box at Kilby Bridge and comes to Wigston, now also alas minus its station, which closed on 18 January 1968.

Top
A fine body of men pause from their labours in haymaking while the photographer records the scene for posterity on a summer day at Great Glen between the wars.

Bottom
Great Glen station is captured for a moment of time in May 1905. Note the carefully tended gardens, a feature of many Midland and other railways' country stations.

Top left
The windmill at Kibworth in a sorry state of neglect. It has now been largely restored and the sails will no doubt turn once more, bringing back one of the now all too rare country sights.

Bottom left
A fine study of compound No. 41032 at the head of an 'up' special as it thunders through the country station of Great Glen.

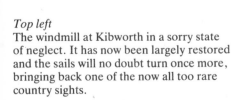

A one-time strong outpost of the stocking and hosiery trade, it was once called Wigston-two-steeples because of its two spired churches standing on the right of the line. An amusing gravestone in the churchyard reads: 'Here lyeth the Remains of Richard Bruin Senior and Goodrith his Wife, aged 152 years, the 21 Anno Dom 1718. "Then Abraham gave up the ghost and died in a good old age full of years and was gathered to his People." Gen 25 Ver 8.' Presumably if Richard did live to be 152 this must be a record for longevity, or were his and his wife's ages added together for the purpose of the tombstone?

Wigston Magna, whose very name reminds us of the Roman influence in this area in early times (its twin village is Wigston Parva, or 'small', which is some ten miles away, and has no connection with its larger brother) was the second largest town in the county in medieval times and had, by the turn of the nineteenth century, a population of 8404, mainly engaged in the manufacture of hosiery.

Wigston was the starting point where the Leicester–Hitchin line sprang from the old Midland Counties Leicester to Rugby line. Almost contiguous was the South Leicestershire line junction which from here carried a branch of the

Top
Revival of an old English custom as a group of Morris dancers perform outside the Greyhound at Great Glen in the early 1950s.

Centre
Midland 0-4-4 tank No. 1369 with a Leicester to Rugby local train near Wigston in 1921.

Bottom
A fine view of Wigston South Junction on 28 June 1947, with the west, or 'Birmingham', curve going off to the left, the locomotive sheds on the extreme right beyond the signal box, and the Midland Counties line to Rugby in the left background behind the water tank.

London & North Western Railway with its own station at Wigston (Glen Parva) southwards through Blaby to Nuneaton. The southern leg of the large triangular junction ran from just north of Wigston Magna station eastwards to join the LNW line after crossing the MCR line at a level crossing just north of a further station at South Wigston on the Rugby line. A further link joined the western end of the triangle directly with the MCR line to Leicester.

By virtue of an Act of 14 June 1860 the Midland obtained running powers between Wigston, Nuneaton and Coventry, and by a further Act passed the following year they obtained powers to make a line from Nuneaton to Whitacre on the old Birmingham & Derby Junction line. Thus direct communication was established between London and Leicester via Wigston into Nuneaton, Birmingham and the West of England.

Because of its importance as an interchange point there were large sidings and a wagon works at Wigston; a locomotive shed was erected in 1873, along with a neat row of houses which provided much-needed accommodation for staff. A number of goods workings were operated from here for which the motive power was usually the standard Midland 0-6-0 goods

Top
A Leicester to Burton local train leaving Knighton Tunnel headed by Deeley 0-6-4 tank No. 2024. This class of locomotives were called 'Flatirons' because of their heavy and ungainly appearance.

Centre
Veteran Midland 2-4-0 No. 25 on an 'up' train south of Leicester in 1925.

Bottom
Exciting moment for the inhabitants of Wigston as the Royal Train, headed by specially turned out Midland 4-4-0 No. 502 with Royal Train headcode, passes by on its way southwards in about 1914.

tender locomotive. In addition to the goods workings there was one 'passenger' turn which involved working the through carriage on the St Pancras to Birmingham service which was detached at Wigston station and taken round the south curve (opened in December 1872) from Wigston Junction to Wigston Glen Parva. This enabled the onward conveyance of the carriage to its destination via the LNWR line to Hinkley and Birmingham. Working this service for many years was an old 0-4-2 well tank which had come to the Midland through the absorption of the Little North Western Railway and had been rebuilt at Derby. Before that the service was worked by the 2-4-0 outside-cylindered tank engine No. 203 built by Robert Stephenson & Company in 1865 for the Wynberg Railway of Cape Town, South Africa, but not taken up. No. 203 was purchased for £1950, and she had worked on the Little North Western line until May 1866 when she was transferred to her new duties, which employed her for twenty years until she was broken up.

The Wigston locomotive shed was closed on 5 November 1934, but was given a new lease of life when the main shed at Leicester was being re-built during the Second World War; it was not finally closed until April 1955.

Leaving Wigston the line passes through lush pasture land, reminding us that the county, particularly in the east, is noted for raising sheep. In 1870 there were half a million sheep in the county with 60 per cent of the farming land given over to pasture. Times have changed since then, and the county now supports roughly equal numbers of sheep and cattle.

Beans were once a main crop in the county, which accounts for the old saying 'Shake a Leicestershire yeoman by the collar and you will hear the beans rattle in his belly'!

From Wigston the line passes Wigston South Junction and Wigston North Junction and in a mile and a half reaches Knighton South and North Junctions which mark the connections of yet another triangular junction – this time with the former Midland line from Burton via Ashby and Coalville now, alas, closed. This line once linked the Leicestershire coalfield villages of Kirkby, Muxloe, Desford, Bagworth and Ellistown, Bardon Hill, Coalville, Swannington,

Ashby, Moira and Gresley by a train service of some eight departures daily in each direction between Burton and Leicester. The line also connected at Desford with the original Leicester & Swannington Railway, opened on 14 July 1832, whose fascinating history lies outside the scope of this book.

Continuing towards Leicester the line enters the 104-yard-long Knighton Tunnel and runs past the single ex-London & North Western Railway platform at Welford Road. This platform served only LNWR line passengers travelling between Nuneaton and Leicester, with trains calling only on Wednesdays and Saturdays for passengers to alight on the 'down' line, and was also used for ticket-collecting purposes; it was closed on 6 February 1918.

Leicester station, some 99 miles from London St Pancras, has recently been completely rebuilt; work on it was finished towards the end of 1982. The station has had a long and varied history, almost as varied as that of the city itself. According to Geoffrey de Monmouth, Leicester was founded by King Lear; modern scholars attribute the name to the old British 'Leir' for the river Soar.

Increasing in size and importance since Roman times, Leicester's population almost trebled in the eighteenth century and the town began to hum with small industry. By 1835 there were 4000 stocking-frames in the town, later added to by the shoe trade and light engineering, and then elastic-web manufacturers, hosiery, lace, tanning, tobacco spinning, wool spinning, brewing and distilling. By 1900 the population had risen to more than 211,000, and the town thus became an increasingly important 'customer' of the Midland Railway.

Leicester became a city in 1919 and was described by the League of Nations in the 1930s as 'Europe's most prosperous city'. It now boasts fine museums, theatres, libraries and exhibition halls and the De Montfort Hall, designed by Lutyens in 1913. Sir Thomas Beecham once remarked tartly, 'The people here don't want music', and indeed the hall is not extensively used. However, the county has a fine schools symphony orchestra, a university, football and rugby clubs, and a much developed city centre with modern shopping precincts alongside the older buildings and its ancient open-air market.

Famous citizens have included 52-stone Daniel Lambert (who died in

Top
One of the last unrebuilt Johnson 4-4-0's with 7ft driving wheels, No. 325, gets into her stride with a train from Leicester to Birmingham in 1921.

Bottom left
Leicester, London Road station on 8 August 1896 clearly showing the all-over roof and other features from the 1892 rebuilding. A Pullman sleeping car stands at the end of the line of stock on the left.

Bottom
An open market and fair in full swing in Humberstone Gate, Leicester in June 1892 is the subject of this Midland advertising photograph.

1809 aged 39) and the legendary old witch of Black Annis Bower in the Dane Hills, who reputedly pounced on children in Leicester forest, ate them and hung their skins on a tree! She no doubt came from Celtic tradition in which magpies were sacred and this saying was spoken aloud when they were sighted:

One for sorrow,
Two for mirth,
Three for a wedding,
Four for a birth.

The original Midland station at Leicester was opened on 4 May 1840 by the Midland Counties Railway Company on a site of nine acres, which the local authorities regarded as 'manifestly absurd in extent'. It became the headquarters of the company with a two-storey station block: public rooms below and offices above. Only one platform, with a loop line and crossover at each end, enabled both 'up' and 'down' trains to be dealt with and allowed through trains to pass.

Opening arrangements were made by a Leicester chemist and druggist, William Evans Hutchinson, who later became a member of the Board and later still chairman of the Midland from 1864 until his retirement in 1870; he remained a Board member until his death in 1882.

The Midland Counties Company promoted the world's first railway excursion – from Nottingham to Leicester's industrial exhibition – which ran on 20 July 1840, fare 6s. (30p) first class, 4s. 6d. (22½p) second class and 2s. (10p) third class (open carriage!). So successful was it that the fourth such excursion, on Monday, 24 August 1840, carried more than 2000 people in one train! Sixty-five coaches were used and two separate engines were sent from Leicester to look for it.

Top
Largely unaltered today, Leicester Midland station as it appeared in about 1905 with horse-drawn tram and omnibus clattering past.

Centre
A crowded scene in the Market Place at Leicester in about 1910.

Bottom
Leicester No. 1 platform on 26 June 1934 as Johnson 2-4-0 No. 207 stands at the head of a train from Kettering. Both engine and coaches had worked through from Cambridge and continued a return working to Kettering via Melton Mowbray.

Having left at 8.30 in the morning, it eventually arrived well after 12.30 p.m.

Thomas Cook of Melbourne, Derbyshire, was seized with the possibilities of these proceedings and became the first private individual to organize an excursion – from Leicester to a Temperance Meeting in Loughborough on 5 July 1841. It carried 570 passengers at a fare of one shilling (5p) each. From this beginning the world-famous travel firm of Thomas Cook & Sons was founded, and it still prospers today.

The original station remained in use until a splendid new four-platform covered station was opened on 12 June 1892, with through lines down the middle and goods lines on the 'up' side. The station was damaged during the Second World War, and deteriorated with time. It has recently been modernized, with new public refreshment facilities, among others.

Leicester, like many other Midland stations, has been famous in the past for its refreshments, and a humorous story is told of a solicitor from St Neots who left the train at Leicester to partake of the services. He returned with a very large portion of pork pie and a flask of sherry. 'Can you digest that?' a fellow traveller inquired sceptically. 'Digest it!' was the reply, 'Do you think, sir, that I allow my stomach to dictate to me what I think proper to put into it?'

By the best trains, Leicester is today a mere 1 hour and 15 minutes from London compared to the Midland's 2 hours and 8 minutes in the 1880s. Apart from trains to St Pancras and Derby, services still run to Birmingham via Nuneaton, and to Nottingham, Peterborough and Norwich.

Top
The 1.50 p.m. from Manchester (Central) to London (St Pancras) with through carriages from Liverpool and Blackburn enters Leicester behind Class 3 4-4-0 No. 702 on 18 September 1909. Leicester engine shed is on the right.

Centre
Edwardian entertainment in Victoria Park, Leicester in about 1907: a brass band entertains the gathered throng from a delightfully ornate bandstand. Brass-band concerts such as this were a very popular form of entertainment, particularly on Sunday afternoons.

Bottom
The proud members of the Midland Railway Leicester Fire Brigade, specially posed as the 1910 winners of the Faire Challenge Trophy.

Just north of the station to the right of the line is the site of the former steam locomotive depot, still used for servicing today's diesel locomotives. From a sixteen-road roundhouse built in early Midland days to replace Midland Counties facilities, a second round shed was added in the 1850s and a third in 1893; the depot was home to most types of Midland engines. A modern roundhouse, proposed before the First World War, was not completed until after the Second World War in 1946! The shed finally closed to steam on 13 June 1966.

Top
Compound 4-4-0 No. 1004, allocated to Leeds, waits in the middle road at Leicester to work forward the 10.00 a.m. Scotch express on 28 December 1909.

Centre
45618 'New Hebrides' stands at No. 3 platform at Leicester with an 'up' express for St Pancras about 1952.

Bottom
A bird's eye view of Leicester station with the newly completed roundhouse in the foreground. This view was commissioned by the contractors, Messrs Tersons, in 1945 after completion of the work.

7
Northwards over the Trent

than a dozen junctions and private sidings joined the line within half a mile.

The next station was Humberstone Road at which local trains called and of which very little now remains. This station once served the nearby northern suburbs of the county town and was closed as an economy measure on 4 March 1968, along with all the other small stations between Leicester and Loughborough.

At the turn of the century Humberstone was a village of some 385 souls. At one time it was noted for the type of coarse alabaster mined nearby but the old village, lying about a mile to the east of the station, has long since been surrounded by the ever-widening boundaries of Leicester itself.

Previous page
A St Pancras–Manchester express crossing the bridge over the Trent just north of Redhill Tunnel behind an ex-Midland Johnson 4-4-0 in rebuilt form piloting a Jubilee class 4-6-0 in about 1954.

As the line leaves Leicester station, it passes on the left the old buildings of the former goods and mineral depots and their associated sidings, once a busy complex and a hive of activity; on the right stands the locomotive establishment referred to in the previous chapter. At one time more

Top
A fine pair of Midland veterans, 2-4-0 No. 62 and 0-6-0 No. 2822 (both double-framed), at the head of a 'down' freight train leaving Leicester in 1923.

Bottom
Humberstone Road station buildings in rather a poor state of repair in April 1967. Closure of the station took place on 4 March 1968.

The line then crosses over the remains of the former Great Northern Company's line from Marefield into its own station at Belgrave Road (closed for passenger traffic on 29 April 1957).

Syston (pronounced 'Syeston'), was once famous for its Leicester-brick cottages, and is a village of considerable antiquity. It had a population of 2930 in 1900, engaged in farming, malting, frame knitting and later shoemaking. The En-Tout-Cas Company, makers of hard tennis-courts, has its headquarters here. Today the village has lost much of its former charm and has been described in recent times as a 'desperately uninviting industrial village'.

Top
4-4-0 No. 40452 at Syston South with a mid-day Peterborough to Leicester train on 6 December 1956.

Centre
A Leicester to Peterborough train of mixed six-wheelers and clerestory bogie carriages entering Syston behind 2-4-0 No. 8 in 1922.

Bottom
Syston village just before the turn of the century, with the usual crowd of onlookers. Note the bread roundsman with the loaves heaped on an open cart and the curious style of angled window-lights in the eaves of the thatched cottages.

Unusual features of Syston church, which is just discernible from the train, are the three figures leaning out from the tower, one-third of the way down – said to represent the founder and his two wives; inside is a carved altar unusually depicting both the wreck of the steamship *Titanic* and Halley's comet!

The station here was of some importance, for it was the main-line junction from which services ran to Melton Mowbray and Peterborough, some 52 miles distant, over the Midland's own route. It was here that a connection was made both with the Great Northern Railway Company's main line and the Great Eastern Company's line to March, as well as with the Midland & Great Northern Joint Railway's line to King's Lynn and beyond. Services from Syston thus enabled passengers from the North to use these routes without the need to go into Leicester.

The first station, to the right of the line, opened on 1 July 1840 and was later replaced in the early 1870s by a second one. This larger station, built to improve facilities for the various branch services, remained open until 4 March 1968.

The Midland line from Syston to Peterborough took a considerable time to complete during the years 1846 to 1848, after the Act giving power to construct it was passed on 30 June 1845. It linked in Melton Mowbray, Oakham, Luffenham and Stamford and was not built without some opposition from Lord Harborough (whose estate lay on the line of the route, at Stapleford Park, Saxby), resulting in various lawsuits between his lordship and the Midland. The section from Syston to Melton Mowbray opened on 1 September 1846 while the other end of the line, between Stamford and Peterborough, opened a month later, on 2 October. However, because of disputes, it was not until 20 March 1848 that the through route was finally opened for coal traffic, and the

Top
A Kettering to Leicester train having run via Melton Mowbray, or 'round the Alps' as it was known, runs into Syston behind 2-6-4 tank No. 42330 in 1957.

Centre
A general view of Syston station looking north.

Bottom
The station buildings at Syston on 15 December 1961.

first passenger service ran on 1 May 1848.

In the early years there was a service of four passenger trains each way on weekdays and two on Sundays; the whole trip of 53 miles took 2½ hours by the best train. Half an hour had been knocked off the journey by 1900 and this remained a standard timing for many years. There was later a through service beyond Saxby to King's Lynn and other places via the Midland & Great Northern Joint line, which brought locomotives from that line into Leicester station.

Beyond Syston on the high ground to the left is Charnwood Forest which remains, in part at least, untouched and extremely beautiful; despite the ever-extending tentacles of modern town and village developments, it is a place of wildness where solitude may still be found. Here the Cistercian monks of Mount St Bernard Abbey remain largely isolated from the pressures of the modern world and pursue their lives of dutiful devotion.

Midway between Syston and Sileby lies the hamlet of Cossington, which was served for a brief period by a station halt named Cossington Gate where one Saturday train in each direction would pause to pick up or to set down passengers. The opening date is not known, but it was in use from at least 1860 and is recorded as having been officially closed from 29 September 1873.

The next station is Sileby (closed on 4 March 1968), of which now only the station house survives. Sileby itself is now an industrial village of red-brick houses, uninspiring in appearance, which was cut in two by the arrival of the Midland line and then joined together again by means of a lofty, two-arch stone overbridge. Sileby church is conspicuous from the railway, with its fine high clerestory showing over the tops of the surrounding houses, while its lofty pinnacled tower soars skyward. In the churchyard is a curious rhyming

Top
Monks at the front of Mount St Bernard's Abbey in about 1910.

Centre
The typical Midland-style wooden station buildings at Sileby as they were in April 1904, with the inevitable advertisement and three milk churns below.

Bottom
The 10.30 a.m. Bradford to St Pancras express at Sileby headed by Leeds (Holbeck) Jubilee No. 45605 'Cyprus'.

High Street, Sileby. 3.

Top
The pleasant High Street at Sileby in the 1950s.

Bottom
A remarkably evocative view of Barrow-on-Soar and Quorn station on a summer day as 2-6-4 tank No. 42181 enters the platform with an 'up' local train.

epitaph to a long-dead sexton, Edward Barradell:

For fifty-two revolving years
Devoutly he attended prayers
With mellow voice and solemn knell
He sang the psalms and tolled the bell.

Next on the line, Barrow-on-Soar station once also served the village of Quorn, from which the most famous Leicestershire hunt (now more than two centuries old) takes its name; the kennels are three miles to the east of the village.

The station was a well-kept place in the nineteenth century, under the ever-watchful eye of stationmaster Welsh. Services amounting to some ten trains each way on weekdays, ran from here southwards to Leicester (for London and the South) and northwards to Loughborough and beyond. In 1903, a third class return to London cost 17s 11d (90p) while first class cost 28s 8d (£1.43).

Originally called merely Barrow, the station was renamed Barrow-on-

Soar in May 1871 and finally became Barrow-on-Soar & Quorn from 1 July 1899. This country halt was, as previously stated, one of the early casualties in 1968, when it and nine other stations on the line were closed. The station did its final business on the last day of 1967, although goods traffic had ceased much earlier, on 6 April 1964.

The village retains a remarkable charm and peace, despite having as near neighbour for centuries the limestone deposits and their associated workings. From these workings, over the years, have been recovered skeletons of our ancestors and of a 20-foot-long plesiosaurus, which is said to have swum in waters here before the dinosaur.

A mile beyond Barrow the line crosses the Soar just after the river divides and flows for some miles on either side of the line. With the widening of this section to provide four tracks, a new portion of bridge was constructed to carry the goods lines and all traffic diverted over this portion while the old MCR bridge was

Top
A view of Barrow-on-Soar village street in the early 1950s.

Centre
The old Midland Counties station buildings at Barrow-on-Soar & Quorn, clearly showing the original lower platform level. View taken in June 1955.

Bottom
Work in progress on the widening of the main-line bridge over the river Soar at Loughborough in 1874. The locomotive is Kirtley straight-framed 0-6-0 No. 347 built by Hawthorn of Newcastle in January 1854.

dismantled and a new one erected to match that on the goods lines. During this work the embankment began to tip and slip into the river. The engineer, John Crossley, hit on an ingenious solution which involved the purchase of several old Trent barges, only good for breaking up, at £4 each. He loaded them with ironstone slag and sank them to form the foot of the embankment, thus obtaining a firm foundation. Close to this point the Soar meets the Trent and so eventually passes to the sea.

Loughborough, 111½ miles from St Pancras, is the second largest town in the county, and was once served by the Midland, L&NW, and Great Central Railways; the embankment which carried the latter over the Midland still stands on the right-hand side as the line runs into the southern end of this station.

The last main line built in the county, the Great Central (which opened for passenger traffic as late as 1 March 1899) was closed on 5 May 1969. The new Great Central Railway – a preservation group – has taken over the Central station in the town together with 5½ miles of track southwards as far as Rothley station; steam trains now operate here at weekends and on bank holidays.

The town of Loughborough is famous for textiles and engineering, and the giant Brush Electrical Engineering works stands to the right of the station. Now part of the Hawker Siddeley group of companies, the firm was founded here as the Falcon Works in 1865 by Henry Hughes, a timber merchant and engineer. He manufactured coaches, wagons, horse-drawn tramcars and tramway engines and, later still, steam locomotives. The firm passed into the hands of the Brush Electrical Engineering Company on 10 August 1889. They began producing electric tramcars and electrical machines at the Falcon Works, turning later to trolley buses,

Top
Loughborough station and the buildings which date back to the rebuilding in the mid 1870s.

Centre
Loughborough still retains its typical Midland awnings but clad in modern sheeting materials, as this 1983 view shows.

Bottom
The north end of Loughborough station in 1890 showing the Brush Falcon Works and the goods lines to the rear of the platforms.

motor cars and omnibuses, and progressing to diesel-electric locomotives: the largest BR class, the Class 47, came from here.

Oldest of the other industries in Loughborough is the bell-founding firm of John Taylor & Co. which has a pedigree going back to 1366, although the name has changed. The firm has cast many great bells in its long history, including (in 1881) 'Great Paul', the 16½-ton, 30-foot giant bell of St Paul's Cathedral. But perhaps their greatest achievement is the revival of the carillon; Loughborough boasts a fine example in its War Memorial which was dedicated on 22 July 1923. The 47 bells were presented by individuals, business firms and corporations in memory of the fallen, and are all appropriately inscribed. At weekends during the summer their mechanical music rings out over the rooftops of the town.

Loughborough itself is an old market town, with a grammar school dating from 1495, and at the turn of the century had a population of some 21,500. The town has been much altered by Victorian additions, including an ancient parish church 'transformed' by Sir Gilbert Scott in a Victorian fashion not generally appreciated today. The town has been considerably extended, and housing estates sprawl outwards in a number of directions; the centre, however, retains a certain limited charm. Rural life affected the town greatly in earlier times; a weekly cattle fair was once held opposite the Volunteer Hotel, and twice-weekly markets were held in the main market place. There was also the annual November Fair, where farm labourers stood and offered themselves for hire for the following year, shaking hands on the deal and receiving a shilling in return. This

Top
A busy scene in the High Street at Loughborough with a crowd of shoppers. Note the sign for the Bull's Head Commercial Hotel and Posting House which straddles the entire street.

Centre
'Milko!' – Norton's farm dairy milk delivery cart in 1909. Such carts were typical and could be seen in the streets of both town and village, dispensing milk by ladle into the customer's own jug. The arrival of bottled milk ended the practice.

Bottom
All the fun of the fair in mid-Victorian times as Wall's Grand Phantoscope drums up custom for possibly a superior type of animated magic-lantern show in the Market Place at Loughborough.

practice continued up to the end of the nineteenth century.

Industries other than those already mentioned included hosiery, dyeworks, brickworks and general engineering. Loughborough's other claim to fame is its University of Technology, the first in England, which began as a small technical institute at the beginning of the twentieth century and now has students from far and wide, involved in technological studies as well as in education and art.

One famous son of the town was Mr Chapman, a mill owner, who invented the hansom cab, while perhaps more famous is Robert Maxwell the sheep breeder, who did much to improve stock in the county.

The original Midland Counties Railway station, opened on 1 July 1840, lay on the opposite side of the Nottingham Road to the present station, which was built as part of the Trent & Leicester widening scheme of 1874–5, when this section of the railway was made four-track to relieve pressure of traffic on the passenger line; the goods lines here pass behind the passenger platforms on the east side.

It was to Loughborough that one of the strangest items of livestock ever was sent – a live gorilla! A Loughborough gentleman with zoological interests had decided that he fancied the idea of keeping a gorilla. However, when the train arrived at Loughborough it was discovered that the beast had slipped from its cage and was loose in the van so, discretion being the better part of valour, it was sent on to the train's final destination which happened to be Nottingham. The chief parcels clerk, foolhardily perhaps, offered to try to recapture it, but to his dismay he discovered that it was bigger than a man and he was bitten in the thigh for his pains! The animal rushed past him

Top
A double-headed 'down' freight train, hauled by 0-6-0's 3496 and 3808, passes through Loughborough station.

Centre
Novel form of traction – the Peebles Steam Car Company's vehicle on trial at Loughborough on 2 June 1905. The Midland already had two steam cars of its own in service on the Morecambe to Heysham line.

Bottom
North of Loughborough, Johnson 2-4-0 No. 222 heads an 'up' stopping train in May 1931.

118

into the street, where a hue and cry ensued – everyone chasing it with sticks and dogs. Eventually, the gorilla was cornered in a timber yard and tackled by the dogs, which were summarily dealt with by several blows from its huge fists. It was not finally restrained until two brave people got a chain and a rope on it. The poor creature was then dutifully conveyed back in disgrace to Loughborough (by Midland Railway of course) and delivered, a little the worse for wear, to its new owner!

This is perhaps the strangest of goods sent by 'parcel', but goods clerks often had to deal with birds and beasts of all kinds – badgers, foxes and even corpses on occasions! The trade in fish, for example, covered everything from small consignments of fish in tins to large consignments of fish sent in huge tanks of salt water, holding perhaps half a ton of live cod. These special fish trains came to Nottingham from Grimsby, via the Manchester, Sheffield & Lincolnshire Railway. The trucks were there sorted and those for London via the Midland line were removed while the remainder continued towards Bristol and elsewhere.

The London market depended very much on cod from Grimsby, and upon arrival at St Pancras the tank of live fish would be lifted off the flat truck by crane and placed on a horse-drawn truck for delivery to the Billingsgate fish market. Empty tanks from the previous day's load were sent back to Grimsby on the return working. En route, at stations like Loughborough, the fried-fish shop owner would purchase a 'kit' or barrel of fresh fish from the fish merchant. Having sold it in halfpenny-worths at a time, he would pay the merchant for it and would settle his debts to the Midland Company with say £15 worth of fishy, green-moulded copper coins, often as much as a man could physically carry.

Half a mile north of Loughborough, just beyond milepost 112, is the place where a further set of water troughs were installed by the Midland, making it possible for a train to pick up 2000 gallons of water in the space of 15 to 20 seconds by means of a lowered scoop, without the need for the driver to slacken speed.

A little further north the line runs near to the village of Normanton-upon-Soar; it was here, in late June 1840, that superintendent Withers of the Midland Counties Railway reported

driver Joseph Barrow and stoker Samuel Dexter 'for being drunk and neglecting the engine, and running it upon the wrong line to the great danger of passengers travelling in an opposite direction'!

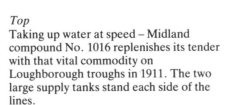

Top
Taking up water at speed – Midland compound No. 1016 replenishes its tender with that vital commodity on Loughborough troughs in 1911. The two large supply tanks stand each side of the lines.

Bottom
Idyllic scene by the river as the church is reflected in the waters at Normanton-on-Soar.

The next station was Hathern, a corruption of 'Hawthorn', and so named because of the abundance of such trees in the parish. It served the village, some 1¼ miles distant across low-lying fields, which had a population of just 114 in 1900. Famous for its pottery, the Hathern Brick & Terra-Cotta Works is still in production today. It was also the home of Mr Heathcoat, a lace manufacturer, who invented technical improvements to bobbin-net machines. When rivals infringed his patents he cut the wages of his staff, some of whom rioted on the night of 28 June 1816 and invaded the factory with blackened faces, smashing fifty-three machines valued at over £6000; in the confusion they shot and killed the nightwatchman, John Asher. Six men were hanged for this crime in front of Leicester jail at noon on 17 April 1817 and three others were transported. Heathcoat removed his business to Devon and so Leicestershire lost its connection with Nottingham lace.

Hathern today remains relatively quiet, in the shadow of the tower of its church which is dedicated to Saint Peter and Saint Paul. The village has a few small businesses, while the station itself, a casualty of changing social circumstances and public habits, was closed to passengers on 1 January 1960, and completely some three days later. Towards the end, only some seven northbound and four southbound local trains called on a weekday and there was no Sunday service.

The line here is on the level and falls only slightly towards Kegworth, opened with the line 1 July 1840. Having crossed the river Soar on the way, the line briefly passes through Nottinghamshire.

Kegworth was once a famous malting and brewing centre, and gypsum was extensively mined in the area. With a population of 2078 at the turn of the century, Kegworth was a lively village. A number of its inhabi-

Top
Hathern church, dedicated to Saints Peter and Paul, stands on a hill overlooking the valley along which the line passes about a mile away.

Centre
Hathern village with half-timbered cottages and the local hostelry. The Three Crowns, off to the right.

Bottom
Sad end for a once-proud Midland station, the Hathern buildings are now used for a very different purpose from that originally intended.

tants are employed at the Midland Agricultural and Dairy College, which still exists under the auspices of Nottingham University. It is a large and well-run training and research centre, placed in superb countryside.

Despite modern pressures, the village remains attractive and largely unspoilt, as modern housing has been well regulated on the fringes. It was from Kegworth station on 30 July 1880 (and no doubt seen off by stationmaster Cross, as a special party) that an excited group set forth, having left their homes at the crack of dawn to be at the station by 6 a.m.: the adult members of the choir from St Anne's Church in nearby Sutton Bonnington (whose long village street runs almost parallel with the line). They were on their annual outing, which this year was to that queen of English seaside resorts, Scarborough. They duly arrived just after 10 a.m., having travelled via York on the Midland and then by North Eastern Railway. After visiting places of interest, some of them ventured into the sea from the bathing huts, while those with a taste for seafood indulged themselves from the many stalls. Some even hardier souls braved a two-hour sail before the party commenced their return journey, arriving back at Kegworth around 11 p.m. No doubt they were all tucked up safely in their Sutton beds before midnight, after reliving the day's events over mugs of cocoa or tea. Just a small event but typical of Midland Railway business in earlier times before the charabanc, and later the special luxury coach and private motor car, took over.

The station survived until 4 March 1968, when it closed to all passenger traffic, although a private siding to the gypsum mines survived a little longer.

The church of Kingston-on-Soar is to the right as the line proceeds northwards. It is said that Anthony Babbington (who was implicated in the plot to murder Elizabeth I and to

Top
Deeley 'Flatiron' 2002 enters Kegworth with a Nottingham to Leicester stopping train.

Centre
The Railway Correspondence and Travel Society Special train at Kegworth on 24 September 1955 with an itinerary that included a trip along the nearby gypsum mines tracks in a train headed by one of the system's locomotives.

Bottom
Kegworth village in January 1983, looking remarkably peaceful.

free Mary, Queen of Scots) hid for two days in the church here, concealed in the massive canopy on top of his kinsmen's tomb, which is covered with figures holding a tub in their hands, representing 'babe in tun' – a pun on the family name.

Next is the little church and village of Ratcliffe-on-Soar, the last village on the line south of the Trent. It was once famous for its abundance of nightingales, all of which must have been frightened away by the coming of the enormous power station which now rears its bell-mouthed cooling towers to the sky. The power station, a short distance from the village that it dwarfs, was opened in 1966 and reached its full 2000-megawatt output in 1969. It is served by a constant flow of merry-go-round trains which provide a non-stop service between the National Coal Board's East Midlands Division pits and the hoppers.

The railway line now plunges into the twin Redhill Tunnels, 154 yards long on the passenger side, 167 yards long on the goods lines and cut, with the aid of gunpowder, through solid alabaster and the red marl which gives the hill its name. Originally consisting of a single bore and built to carry the original two Midland Counties lines through the hill towards Leicester, the tunnel was given a second matching bore in 1899 which carries a pair of goods lines and thus removes the congestion of traffic at this point.

Both tunnel mouths at the northern end boast porticos and castellated towers, and there is a legend that a nineteenth-century land owner, determined to extract his just dues from the Midland for the passage of trains over his land, sat in the tallest tower of the old tunnel and counted the trains that passed along the line below. In fact the rooms concealed within the turrets were originally used by railway policemen and other servants keeping watch on the lines below.

As the railway line emerges from the tunnel it almost instantly crosses the river Trent by means of a fine

Top
Gypsum Mines Ltd 0-4-0 saddle tank 'Lady Angela' on the private system during a rail tour on 29 August 1935.

Centre
Where nightingales once sang – the village of Ratcliffe-on-Soar.

Bottom
A fine pair of horses, possibly Midland dray horses, in about 1890.

three-arched bridge, each arch having a span of 100 feet. The bridge was built from ironwork supplied by the Butterley Company (makers of the main roof girders of St Pancras station) from their ironworks near Ripley, Derbyshire, and work commenced in June 1839. The piers and abutments are of stone and at the north end are two arches, each with 25-foot span, over the Cranfleet Cut built to carry floodwaters more easily past this obstruction. A second bridge was built in 1899 to carry the new goods lines.

The Trent, third longest river of England, is joined just before this point by its tributaries the Derwent and the Soar, and as a navigable waterway it has figured largely in the history of this part of the country. It remains tidal as far as Gainsborough in Lincolnshire for vessels up to 200 tons.

The river gave its name to Trent station, once situated 119 miles 65 chains from St Pancras, but alas now gone. Trent station was opened on 1 May 1862, although it was not finally completed until some time later. Being situated just to the east of the junction of the lines from Leicester and Derby on their way to Nottingham, Trent, in its heyday, was one of the most important junctions on the Midland system, with lines branching off in every direction. In Midland Counties days a simple triangle was formed linking the Derby to Nottingham, Nottingham to Leicester and Derby to Leicester lines, but at that time there was no station.

The next stage involved the Midland's thrust up the Erewash Valley from South Erewash Valley Junction to Codnor Park, and the construction of the curve from Long Eaton Junction to North Erewash Junction, opened on 6 September 1847. This completed a second triangular junction, which crossed the Derby–Nottingham line on the level at Platt's Crossing.

Top
Completing the new viaduct to carry the separate goods lines over the river Trent north of Redhill Tunnel in 1899.

Centre
The twin bridges over the Trent as seen from Redhill Tunnel; passenger lines on the left and freight lines on the right.

Bottom
The second Redhill Tunnel, an exact replica of the original, and built to carry the new freight lines, nearing completion in 1899.

The third stage, brought into operation with the opening of Trent station itself, included the opening of a second Long Eaton station, this time situated on the Erewash Valley line. Connecting lines from Trent station South Junction to Sheet Stores Junction came into being; the original Long Eaton station was closed and demolished and the direct line from there to Platt's Crossing became a dead-end siding.

Lord Grimthorpe described the important interchange station thus:

You arrive at Trent. Where it is I cannot tell. I suppose it is somewhere near the River Trent, but then the Trent is a very long river. You get out of your train to obtain refreshment, and having taken it, you endeavour to find your train and your carriage. But whether it is on this side or that, and whether it is going north or south, you cannot tell. Bewildered, you frantically rush into your carriage; the train moves off round a curve and then you are horrified to see some lights glaring in front of you and you are in immediate expectation of a collision, when your fellow passenger calms your fears by telling you that they are the tail lamps of your own train!

Trent was certainly a puzzle to both strangers and regular travellers alike in early years; for planted on either side of the single-island platform stood an identical row of trees. Trains arrived from either direction and those from Derby, by using two different curves, could arrive facing towards Nottingham or London. It was well known that when John Elliott was superintendent of the line he wished to close Trent altogether and transfer passengers at Attenborough, Long Eaton or Kegworth. Trent became so famous that local folk still say 'Well, I'll go to Trent' when faced with an unbelievable situation.

The refreshment room was run in Victorian times by former Derby

Top
The confusing station at Trent clearly showing the two lines of trees and almost identical sides to the station buildings as it appeared to passengers on 8 August 1896 in this Midland official photograph.

Centre
Much of the glass roofing is missing in this view of Trent taken on 12 June 1947; Midland 2P 4-4-0 No. 556 heads a stopping train for Nottingham.

Bottom
A view which shows the convenience of the north curve at Trent as compound No. 41077 enters the station on a Derby–St Pancras excursion in 1953.

barmaid Miss Luscott, generally known as 'Ma', who had been a belle in her younger days and who provided the best of homely fare.

William Taylor was a noted station-master who tapped with a carriage key on the stone window-sill of his office while awaiting the next arrival; a habit which, over the years, resulted in deep holes which had to be patched with cement to restore the stonework to an acceptable appearance!

From 1870 onwards, operating costs on the London Extension had been cleverly reduced by forming combined trains which ran as far as Trent (and in some cases Derby) before being separated in order to complete their respective journeys. In the opposite direction the reverse was true, and Trent became the focal point for through carriages from Liverpool, Manchester and the West Riding of Yorkshire, which were suitably combined for working up to St Pancras as single units. Of course, good timekeeping was of the essence so that the complex operation could run like clockwork, and Midland drivers had their wages docked by the exaction of fines for unnecessary delays.

Trent's importance as an interchange station was much diminished by the opening of the Kettering, Manton and Nottingham line, which provided an alternative through route from London to the North and gave an opportunity for running the fastest expresses with the minimum of stop-pages. However, the station survived as an intermediate stopping point for the Derby and Leicester to Nottingham local services, and some expresses to London from the North, Derby and Nottingham continued to call there for connection purposes into the early 1960s.

Top
Trent served Long Eaton, as well as being an interchange point, and this view, taken about 1914, shows Derby Road with carts and bicycles much in evidence, and a lady of ample proportions on the right!

Centre
Train approaching Sawley Junction station headed by Class 2P 4-4-0 No. 537. On the left are the Midland's Sheet Stores, where wagon sheets were made, repaired and marked with the Midland's own distinctive colour coding and pattern.

Bottom
Sawley Junction station (now Long Eaton) as seen from a signal looking north. The station buildings are on the road below right. The view was taken on 7 February 1957.

Draycott Station.

The station was closed on 1 January 1968 and was completely demolished. All that survives now is the row of railway houses adjacent to the new Trent power signal box which controls traffic over a wide area.

No matter which route was taken from Trent towards Derby, the line eventually arrived at Sawley Junction where the north curve from Trent (now lifted) rejoined the main line to Derby. The direct route from Trent passed the former Midland Railway Company's 'Sheet Stores' after which the nearby junction from Trent is named. Here the Midland had a works of some size engaged in the manufacture and repair of tarpaulins and sheeting for the protection and safe carriage of open-wagon loads of all kinds of substances.

The station here, originally Sawley Junction, was renamed Long Eaton when the old Long Eaton (second) station on the Erewash Valley main line was closed to passenger traffic on 2 January 1967, although the former station was much nearer the centre of the town; the present Long Eaton station is at the extreme western end of this quite important town. Long Eaton is now very much residential, but its once-thriving industry included the wagon works of S. J. Claye, the extensive Toton goods-marshalling sidings which at one time handled up to 26,000 wagon loads a day, and the lace works of Messrs Fletcher. In the middle of the nineteenth century more than fifty machines were employed in lace production in the town.

Slightly nearer to Derby stood Sawley station, 121 miles 42 chains from St Pancras, which was called Breaston in Midland Counties days, but renamed within a year because of confusion with Beeston on the line to Nottingham only 5½ miles away. It was closed on 1 December 1930,

Top
Draycott station in Midland days with a dip in the platform to provide a barrow crossing. This station served both Draycott to the left and Breaston to the right.

Centre
The employees of Plackett's lace mill at Breaston about 1888 with experienced hands lining up with some very young apprentices.

Bottom
Time for a family drive as chauffeur James Bird holds open the rear door of the tonneau body on the 1903 12h.p. Napier for Mr Marcus Astle, his wife and daughters to enter at the back of their home, Atwell House in Station Road, Draycott.

another victim of changing social habits.

The line now reaches the site of Draycott station, opened with the Midland Counties line to Nottingham. It was renamed Draycott and Breaston on 7 August 1939 in recognition of the fact that the spread of housing around the latter brought residents within an easy walk of the station. It was closed on 14 February 1966.

The station lies at the eastern end of the village, and the line runs across its north-east side. A cotton mill was established here in 1800 and a lace factory with 40 machines in 1842, following the 'opening up' by the railway. Other mills followed, notably the Victoria Mills of Jardines built in 1906.

Borrowash has had two stations in its life and has now lost them both! The first stood on the banks of a cutting 25 feet high and was opened with the line on 30 May 1839 as a 'temporary affair'. It closed on 1 May 1871 in favour of a new one, built on a site a quarter of a mile to the west and called Borrowash & Ockbrook until 1 April 1904. The station served the two small villages of those names lying to the east of the line. The new station (and the railway line at this point) is sandwiched between the Derby Canal, lying behind a stone wall some 25 feet higher at this point, and the river Derwent lying below and to the left.

The village of Borrowash (a corruption of 'burrow ash') has little of significance in its history, except that it was once the location of an ancient cornmill which stood on the Derwent and belonged to nearby Dale Abbey. Many of the inhabitants were formerly employed in a cotton mill built by Messrs Towle, which also lay on the river, but many of today's inhabitants commute by car and bus to Derby or Nottingham, while some work at the nearby plant of Courtaulds Acetate.

Top
The Moravian settlement at Ockbrook, founded in 1750 and one of only three in the country. Its girls' school still provides a good education.

Centre
A Midland dray decorated for Ockbrook Cycle Parade on 22 June 1912. Note the driver's Official Midland Railway hat and the splendidly turned out decorated harness on the well-groomed horse.

Bottom
Borrowash station on 29 July 1923, with London, Tilbury & Southend section 4-4-2 tank No. 2118 and a new rake of close-coupled coaches on a trial run from Derby.

On the other hand, Ockbrook, a little further from the line on the opposite side of Borrowash, is famous as being one of only three Moravian settlements in England. Its girls' school, founded in 1750, still flourishes.

Borrowash station was always inconvenient for Ockbrook, and with the growth of other modern forms of transport its usefulness to the local inhabitants went into decline. It lost its goods services on 4 January 1965, and closed completely, with Draycott and Breaston, on 14 February 1966.

The line now reaches Spondon, the last station on the line before Derby. Here right next to the station on our left lies the giant works of Courtaulds Acetate (known until 1957 as British Celanese), specializing in man-made fibres and other chemical products.

The village of Spondon lies some distance away to the right on top of a hill overlooking the river valley. The spire of its ancient St Werburgh's church, founded in Saxon times and rebuilt after a fire in 1340, rises gracefully over the roofs of the eighteenth-century brick houses which form the old village, and above the modern sprawling housing estates that lie all around it.

Spondon station itself was not completed in time for the opening of the Midland Counties line but was eventually opened for traffic under stationmaster Carter's supervision, on 11 November 1839. Thereafter five trains from both Derby and Nottingham called at the station daily, the first class return fares then being 1s. (5p) and 3s. (15p) respectively.

Leaving Spondon the line swings to the left, leaving the former Chaddesden sidings and the old Midland Counties line to Derby on the right, and approaches the city from the south-east.

Top
Nottingham Road, Borrowash looking towards Derby about 1905.

Centre
Spondon station on 19 June 1954, with Class 5 4-6-0 No. 44661 heading the 12.5 p.m. Derby to London (St Pancras) express. Apart from the two station platforms on the main line, works trains were booked to call in the platform at the left of the picture.

Bottom
The level crossing at Spondon giving access to the British Celanese works, seen from the Derby Canal bridge on 20 November 1924. The unusually large signal box controlled the sidings, the level crossing and the main station traffic.

8
Derby–
headquarters of the Midland

Until the railway arrived Derby was a prosperous market town, with a history dating back to before Roman times. Derby is celebrated for its porcelain, and for being the place where the first English silk mills and calico mills were founded, the former by John Lombe, the latter by Arkwright. There were some engineering and other manufacturing works here before the arrival of the Midland, but the coming of the railways to the town changed the direction of progress and set it on a path which brought much new industrial development and population growth. The technological advances which flowed from some of the firms who were attracted to the town have made Derby famous the world over.

Daniel Defoe, who visited the town,

Previous page
The oldest known view of Derby works and station, taken in 1860, with the first round-house of 1840 and the North Midland workshops in the foreground, the single platform station with train shed beyond and a smoky town in the distance.

Bottom
Derby station and locomotive works seen from the engineer's offices at the north end of platform No. 1. Additional platforms, Nos. 2, 3, 4, 5 (bay) and 6, have been added since the view on p. 129 was taken.

styled it 'one of gentry rather than of trade', but within a century all this was to change.

Our first chapter related the events which led to the town being adopted as a terminus by three separate railway companies, the Midland Counties, the North Midland, and the Birmingham & Derby Junction, each of which had independent workshops or sheds near the station.

Under Matthew Kirtley's direction as Locomotive and Carriage and Wagon Superintendent, the separate parts were welded into a single unit, eventually capable of building locomotives, carriages, and wagons. To the original North Midland workshops, with their central roundhouse, two further roundhouses were added in 1847 and 1852 respectively. The workshop accommodation was gradually extended and improved to enable more and more work to be undertaken by the company itself in order to be better able to meet the requirements of the ever-enlarging Midland system. The building of a large new block was approved in April 1872. This was to comprise erecting, machine and paint shops, but Kirtley died on 24 May 1873 before the work was completed. It was left to his successor, Samuel Waite Johnson (who came to the

Midland from the Great Eastern Railway) to oversee the final stages.

At this point in its history, however, the Midland decided to separate the locomotive and the carriage and wagon appointments, and Thomas Gething Clayton came to Derby from Swindon, where he had had oversight of the building of the new Great Western Railway carriage and wagon shops, to repeat the exercise for the Midland. Whereas the old locomotive works had been adjacent to the station, a brand new site of some 50-odd acres was chosen on the opposite side of the main London 'direct' line. This had been opened on 27 June 1867 so that trains from London to Manchester and the North would not have to change direction at Derby; before that date all trains used the old Midland Counties line, which passed through the Chaddesden goods sidings, and approached the station from the north end by means of a sharp curve, meeting the old North Midland line to the north just before it crossed the Five Arches bridge over the Derwent.

A plan for the new workshops, with a ground area of 12 acres, was approved in December 1873, one month after purchase of the site, and by July 1877 the extensive new

Carriage & Wagon works was in full production. Everything was planned on a large scale: foundations took a year to dry out, prodigious quantities of brick, ironwork and timber were needed, and the space between the sides of buildings was kept at 85 feet, leaving room for five lines of rails. Space between building ends was 70 feet, which enabled the works to construct the longest vehicles necessary until into the 1970s; after that some of the shops had to be slightly reduced in length to make enough space to traverse modern 21-metre-long coaches sideways between the buildings.

Top
Group of shop foremen at Derby Locomotive Works about 1872, grouped around Kirtley 0-6-0 No. 321 built there in June 1859.

Centre
The Derby Carriage & Wagon works carriage repair shop about 1890 with a variety of stock. Note the hydraulic lifting devices for bodies and the bogies under construction.

Bottom left
Matthew Kirtley, the first Locomotive, Carriage & Wagon Superintendent of the Midland, in office from 13 June 1844 until 24 May 1873 when he died.

Bottom right
Samuel Waite Johnson, Kirtley's successor as Locomotive Superintendent from 1 July 1873 until his retirement on 31 December 1903. Johnson was responsible for some of the most aesthetically pleasing steam locomotive designs ever produced.

Modern developments have included the further expansion of the London Midland & Scottish Railway's original research laboratories set up by Sir Harold Hartley in 1932, which have now become a part of today's Railway Technical Centre, the first phase of which was opened by HRH Prince Philip on 14 May 1964. The complex now houses centralized research, design, purchasing, supplies and workshops headquarters facilities for the British Railways Board and British Rail Engineering Limited.

A School of Transport, opened by the LM & SR in 1938 as a residential school for some 50 students, still functions; its brief is now extended to cater for 1000 persons on a variety of training courses every year.

The first stations at Derby were two temporary affairs, for plans were already in hand to provide a joint station for all three companies, meeting in the town. The Midland Counties Railway opened for business on 4 June 1839 from a wooden station building just north of the bridge over the river Derwent, while the Birmingham & Derby Junction Railway Company began operating from a similar building near to the London Road on 12 August 1839 after an official opening the week before.

The new joint station, built by the North Midland Railway Company, with the other two companies contributing 6 per cent per annum towards the cost of their particular accommodation, was brought into use for the first time on 11 May 1840, with the opening of their line to Rotherham. At this time the other two temporary stations were closed.

Top
The old front of Derby station as it was in 1891 before the present frontage was added and the porte-cochère relocated in front of it.

Centre
The best of fare is carried in appealing display on this Midland platform refreshment barrow on Derby station on 23 February 1908. Bovril and hot milk are available as well as the best wines and, of course, Schweppes' table waters.

Bottom
The interior of Derby station about 1902 with ladies in elegant period dress on platform No. 4 as a Bristol express is about to depart.

132

It was described by the *Illustrated London News* on 15 July 1843 as 'the first by universal consent in the Empire or indeed the world. Its prodigious extent, its incomparable plain form, its light but beautiful roof, its refreshment room, its fine hotel, and the admirable manner in which its immense transactions are conducted must fill every stranger with surprise and admiration'. Built to the design of Francis Thompson at a cost of £130,000, it was thought at the time to be much too large for any future traffic. The main façade was a full 1050 feet long, dominated by a boldly projecting central block with a Venetian window above the main entrance. The three-bay glazed train shed, 34 feet high to the apexes, was supported on sixty graceful reeded and bonded 22-foot-high cast-iron columns, which also served as rainwater pipes. The single platform ran the full length of the façade but had inset faces at the north and south ends enabling the Midland Counties and the Birmingham & Derby Junction trains to stand there, while the North Midland trains could enter and leave from the central projecting face. A number of turntables were set into these platform faces, enabling vehicles to be transferred from the platforms to any of the other seven through lines, some of which were used for stock storage and the loading and unloading of goods. Some of the turntable lines ran through the outside curtain wall of the train shed and permitted direct access to the engine roundhouse and other facilities lying within the North Midland workshops area.

Over the years the station was enlarged by the addition of two further island platforms, each with two main faces; the largest alteration was for the Royal Agricultural Show held in Derby in 1881, when platforms No. 4, 5 (bay) and 6 were added to cope with the increased traffic.

Top
Johnson single No. 644 piloting compound 4-4-0 No. 1058 get into their stride leaving Derby with a Manchester (Central) to London (St Pancras) express about 1924.

Bottom
Old friends bid each other farewell at Derby station in this delightful Edwardian period photograph taken in about 1906.

The station survived serious bomb damage to one section during the Second World War, and little other major work was done until, in 1952, a £200,000 modernization plan was put in hand which resulted in the complete demolition of the old train shed and the erection of individual roofing on reinforced concrete pillars and framing for each island platform with a new central footbridge. The work was completed in July 1954. However, time has not dealt kindly with the modern mode of building and today, less than thirty years on, a £3 million scheme is being undertaken to modernize the station yet again. This time all that remains of the old station buildings and the porte-cochère will be swept away, although it has to be said that they are perhaps in better shape than the modern platform canopies of the early 1950s!

Station characters have abounded over the years and it is appropriate to look at a few at this point.

George Henry Rickman, who was stationmaster in early Midland days, lived for a number of years in a whitewashed cottage specially built for him on the lineside near London Road bridge. He met his death on 1 November 1866 at Derby North Junction on the first day that trains began running through Derby via Chaddesden sidings without calling at the station. In a moment's forgetfulness he stood in the path of the new non-stop train and paid with his life. His death caused a great sensation and there was a very large and imposing funeral.

James Maxey, from Sheffield, took over the position, and he is best remembered for his staff interviews, which were many and frequent. On one occasion a porter had made a complaint and requested an interview at which Maxey commented, 'So you are not satisfied? You come to us without a rag to your back or a penny in your pocket, we feed you, we clothe you, we put money in your purse and bread in your mouth, and still you complain. The best thing for you to do is to scuttle off as fast as you can.'

The Midland's first head booking clerk was Edward Clulow. It was a coveted position, for it carried with it the right to live at 23 Railway Terrace in a block of company houses, opposite the station itself. To hold the keys was regarded as a pinnacle of achievement, experienced by few only. Before W. H. Smith & Sons obtained the sole trade as booksellers and newsagents, Clulow was allowed to carry on his trade both on the station and at his house. He afterwards became district postmaster in Midland Road, leading from the station, and the Midland purchased all their stamps from his establishment. He also kept a fine shop nearby with stationery in one window and china in the other. He later moved to Victoria Street and, although the family is no longer connected with it, his name is still commemorated in a bookshop near the cathedral.

Robert Bartlett was another 'arresting' character; he was the tall policeman who looked after the station frontage. He was nicknamed 'Hall-door Bob' and it was said that he could get a larger tip for handling an umbrella than a porter could for moving a whole pile of luggage. One night, after a visit to Nottingham, he mistakenly got out of the train at the ticket platform on Five Arches bridge and somehow survived a fall into the swiftly flowing waters of the Derwent twenty feet below. While on the subject of tips, we should refer to 'fluffing' and 'weaseling'. The former referred to a man coming on to the platform to carry luggage when not actually on

Bottom
Class 3 4-4-0 No. 758 makes a spirited start from No. 4 platform at Derby with a Bristol-bound express in about 1912.

duty as a porter, to the detriment of those porters already there; 'weaseling' was the practice of staying over time or coming on to the platform in off-duty moments for extra tips.

Chief of the railway police was Edward ('Ned') Farmer who had once been a Bow Street Runner and looked every inch the part. He was a quaint character, bubbling over with humour and full of funny stories, but he kept to the letter of the law, and he travelled in every day from Tamworth. He died on 10 July 1876 and is buried in the churchyard there with a suitable quotation from his favourite poem 'Little Jim' inscribed on his monument.

Top
Compound 4-4-0 No. 1057 enters Derby from the London line about 1924. Note the signal gantry with separate signals for Nos. 1, 2 and 3 platforms.

Centre
A mixed bag of motive power at Derby in 1922 with (left to right) a Johnson 2-4-0, a London & North Western 0-6-0 on a train for Walsall and Birmingham, and a Class 2P 4-4-0 No. 433 in platform No. 4.

Bottom
The North Staffordshire Railway also used Derby, as shown here by the presence of 2-4-0 No. 54 leaving platform No. 2 with a local train for Stoke about 1912.

One of the most fascinating departments of a large railway station such as Derby was the lost-luggage office. Some lost items such as gloves, handkerchiefs and umbrellas are understandable, but F. S. Williams records the following oddities left behind in mid Victorian times: a pair of leather hunting-breeches, a complete set of soldier's kit; a set of bagpipes; a 'very superior' astronomical telescope; a feather bed; a galvanized iron copper; a large oil painting; a cask of cement; a perambulator; a pair of crutches; and a wooden leg!

As for traffic, Derby was of course at the very centre of the Midland's system, lying as it does at the intersection of the north to south and north-east to south-west main routes. From the south came expresses originating from St Pancras bound for Manchester by means of the glorious route through the Derbyshire Peak District, and thence to Liverpool; alternatively by branching off at Ambergate one could reach Chesterfield, Sheffield and all points north, including Leeds, and thence on to the spectacular scenic route over the Settle–Carlisle line to Scotland. South-westwards, using the former Birmingham & Derby Junction line, one could reach Bristol and all points beyond while, in addition, there were local services to Nottingham and Lincoln and thence the east coast, or to Stoke and Crewe via the North Staffordshire line and on to North Wales.

Of course, apart from these main routes there were the local branch lines to Ripley, Wirksworth and Melbourne, while the London & North Western and North

Top
The cattle docks just north of Derby station served the adjacent market, as shown in this early-morning scene on 26 November 1909. A little further north stood the other Derby Midland station at Nottingham Road.

Centre
Beyond the Nottingham Road station is the busy goods yard at St Mary's, as this view illustrates, with a pair of hand-cranes loading a Rolls-Royce Silver Ghost chassis onto a railway vehicle for a journey to the bodymakers. The photograph was taken on 26 June 1911.

Bottom
Derby station by gaslight showing platforms Nos. 3 & 4 with Johnson 2-4-0 No. 133 on station pilot duties and the platforms littered with masses of milk churns. View taken in April 1908.

Staffordshire companies both worked traffic into the town, and the NSR had their own locomotive depot adjacent to the London Road.

Also, quite apart from passenger traffic there was a huge volume of miscellaneous goods and mineral traffic to be dealt with, moving in and out of the Midland's main goods depot at Derby St Mary's, just beyond the Nottingham Road station. Traffic included iron and steel, coal, timber and a variety of other raw materials, together with finished manufactured items departing by goods train to all parts.

Milk traffic at Derby was also very important at one time for, with charges of only a halfpenny a gallon for short distances and a penny for long ones, Derbyshire farmers found it well worth their while to send milk even to distant cities on the Midland lines. From the rich meadow lands around Duffield, Ripley, Wirksworth and Castle Donnington, farmers would send their milk by the earliest morning local trains to Derby and by six o'clock in the evening the centre platforms at Derby would be crowded with churns. The morning train would regularly leave for London shortly after 8 a.m. with as many as eight or ten vans each containing 40 churns holding some 15 gallons apiece. From the 1880s until the early part of the twentieth century the traffic continued, and was only gradually replaced by road transport, local co-operative dairies and bottling plants.

Beyond the station, over the Five Arches bridge across the Derwent, lay the Midland's own signal works, which began in quite a small way but grew to employ over 800 men, 500 of whom were at Derby. The works manufactured some 1200 signals each year, ranging from the usual signals of 45 feet or so in height to the tallest some 65 feet high, of which six feet were set in the ground. Also manufactured were the signal boxes,

Top
Royal Scot class 4-6-0 No. 46116 'Irish Guardsman' sets off for the north with an express over the Five Arches bridge. On the left is the Midland signal works.

Centre
Stanier Class 5 4-6-0 No. 45280 approaches Derby from the west with a special from Birmingham in July 1959.

Bottom
Now preserved, Jubilee class 4-6-0 No. 45690 'Leander' stands at No. 6 platform at Derby on 19 August 1951 with a Bradford to Bristol express.

including planking, boarding, window sashes, steps and galleries as well as the variety of ironwork involved.

Immediately opposite the station stands the historic Midland Hotel, one of the first purpose-built railway hotels in the world. It was built as a private venture at the same time as the original station and has recently been taken over by Midland Hotels Limited who have lavished some £150,000 on its redevelopment and restoration to the original style. Originally known as Cuff's Hotel, it became Midland property on 1 March 1862 and since that date has been extended and altered several times. Queen Victoria stayed at the hotel in 1849 and visited it again on 21 May 1891 for a banquet given by the mayor and corporation. Its huge cellars extend right underneath the station itself; it was from here that the huge quantity of wines and spirits bottled by the Midland Company found their way not only into the famous luncheon baskets supplied to passengers en route but to every part of the Midland system where a refreshment room could be found. Alas, today these cellars stand desolate and empty – not a vestige of Napoleon brandy, or indeed vin rouge, remains to testify to their glorious past!

The area around the station, formerly fields until the arrival of the railway, was soon developed with houses to provide accommodation of varying standards for the employees of the Midland, depending on their status. In those days a man in charge

Top
The Midland Hotel at Derby, built at the same time as the station as a private venture but acquired by the Midland in 1862. It has received many visitors of note, including royalty, during its long history. This view was taken in 1899.

Centre
The recently restored Midland houses in Calvert Street (formerly North Street), which have been rescued from demolition (along with two other rows, two side streets and courts) by the efforts of Derby Civic Society and the Derbyshire Historic Buildings Trust. This housing adjacent to the station provided accommodation for key Midland personnel, many of whom were 'on call' by bell for instant duty if required.

Bottom
A good old-fashioned corner shop, near to the Locomotive Works, which provided a wide range of groceries and other provisions; next door stands the Derby Steam Laundry and the 'Success' Cigar and Tobacco store.

of an office or some other group of staff would receive a salary of some £150 per annum; such an employee was an important person, able to live in the better type of house in High Street, Oxford Street, Regent Street, Morleston Street or on the Osmaston Road itself.

Nearby one could partake of the delights of the Arboretum, laid out by Loudon and presented to the town by Joseph Strutt, a mayor of Derby; it was opened on 16 September 1840. This, the first public park in England, was tastefully laid out with winding paths among grassy slopes and flower beds, with fountains, statuary and a small zoo. It was the resort of many families in the summer evenings or on a Sunday, when brass bands would play selections from the popular music of the time while parents strolled or sat and children bowled hoops or skipped to the music.

Other industries of the town were prospering after the arrival of the railway, and even more were later attracted to the town by the excellent

The Fountain Arboretum, Derby

Top
The Derby Arboretum was a popular resort for local inhabitants with its tree-lined walks, fountains, flower beds and at one time, a small zoo and aviary.

Bottom
The Rolls-Royce car production line at the Nightingale Road factory, Derby about 1920.

facilities offered by the station's situation, commanding good routes to all points of the compass. Rolls-Royce came to the town in 1908 and built a works on the Osmaston Road: from Henry Royce's inspired idea of making a car out of the best materials to the highest possible standards of workmanship, has come a continuing story of high achievement which has run through cars and aircraft engine design, such as the Silver Ghost car and the Merlin aero engine, right up to today's modern high-technology gas-turbine aero engines such as those in the RB211 range.

Other Derby firms with high-standing reputations throughout the world include Aiton & Co. Ltd which designs and manufactures high-quality pipework for power stations and desalination plants for converting sea water to fresh water; Crompton Cables, who produce elastomeric and thermoplastic cables for world-wide use; International Combustion Ltd which supplies large steam-generating units and specialized pipeline and mechanical handling equipment; Birmid Qualcast Ltd, with a history dating back to 1901, producing precision high-quality castings for the motor trade as well as lawn mowers, and Fletcher & Stewart Ltd, world-wide suppliers of processing plant for cane and sugar beet as well as refining and distilling equipment.

Fine bone china and porcelain have been made in Derby since 1748 and the city is, of course, the home of

Royal Crown Derby china; Queen Victoria granted the prefix 'Royal' to the firm's name in 1890. Today it continues to manufacture its distinctive high-quality named products at the Osmaston Road factory, although the firm now forms part of the Royal Doulton Tableware Group.

Joseph Mason began producing materials for the paint trade in quite a small way at the beginning of the nineteenth century, and because of their high reputation among builders of coaches and stately carriages, it was natural that the Midland Company should use these local products for the painting of its carriages, rolling stock and locomotives. This has resulted in the steady growth of the firm to its present seven-acre site on the Nottingham Road, and the world-wide fame of its products.

Another business which profited from the arrival of the Midland Railway in the town was that of William Bemrose. He began business in nearby Wirksworth in October 1826 but in 1827 took the opportunity to move to Derby, where he set up business as a stationer, bookseller and printer. The arrival of the railways in the town gave Bemrose his golden opportunity, which he seized with both hands, first becoming printer to the North Midland Company and then to its successor, the Midland Railway itself. A steady growth in the printing side then began, for the firm not only produced timetables, stationery and leaflets of all kinds for the Midland

Above
Derby station in September 1921, with an early taxi-cab and its predecessors, the horse-drawn cabs of the Victorian era, awaiting hire. In the left background is the Midland Railway Institute, providing all employees with a variety of activities including a library, reading room, dining room and assembly halls for dances and other social gatherings.

and other companies, but started to print its own railway guides in July 1847. By 1884 the Midland alone needed some 35,000 timetables each half-year, which incidentally were sold at one penny but cost fourpence each to print. From these early beginnings the Bemrose firm continued to grow and widen its product range, improving the technology of its printing processes. After a long history in a large factory opened near the station, its modern factories in Derby and Spondon now produce a wide range of printing and packaging materials.

The Midland Railway in each case gave an impetus to the business development of the various firms by providing new marketing opportunities in places further afield than their traditional ones.

Derby's population, already a thousand strong in AD 1000, had risen to 11,000 by 1800 and by the beginning of the twentieth century there were some 115,000 inhabitants, no fewer than 10,000 of whom were employed by the Midland. Today the population stands at nearly 240,000.

The town retained its mayor and its borough status at the local government

Top left
An early bill printed by William Bemrose & Sons advertising a Midland picnic with a variety of intriguing activities. The 'Jingling Match' deserves some explanation: there were usually about ten competitors, one of whom had bells attached to his knees and elbows. The others were blindfolded. A match lasted about half an hour and if the jingling player could evade his pursuers for that period he was deemed to be the winner. Otherwise the prize went to his captor.

Top right
Irongate, Derby about 1860, with All Saints church (later Derby Cathedral) in the distance. The original Derby shop of William Bemrose is at the extreme left-hand side with three old time 'peelers' standing just beyond.

Bottom
A group of Midland station staff from Derby with a young lady, about 1910.

reorganization of 1972, and Her Majesty Queen Elizabeth II was pleased to confer city status on Derby by Letters Patent in her Jubilee year of 1977.

Much of the old town, as it was before the coming of the railways, has been swept away; for although the city did not suffer destruction by bombs during the Second World War like other Midland cities, the often unsteady hands of the town planners have not left the city unscathed. Whereas other cities have managed to retain the old in harmony with and alongside the new, Derby has been careless with its ancient parts and the present admixture of modern, Victorian and earlier architecture is not a happy one. A few charming corners remain and are now being conserved, but Derby has lost much of its traditional spirit and flavour, and its citizens now have a struggle to identify themselves with what it has become.

Its saving grace rises above the city like a timeless sentinel in the shape of the magnificent 212-foot-high tower of the cathedral church of All Saints, completed in 1527. It is now somewhat unhappily married to a much later church building, designed by James Gibbs and of a different architectural form and period, which was erected in 1727. It was enlarged between 1966 and 1972 by the addition of a retrochoir, chapter room, song school and other accommodation, well designed by Sebastian Comper. Inside there is much of interest including a wrought-iron screen by Robert Bakewell and the monument to Elizabeth, Countess of Shrewsbury (better known as Bess of Hardwick), who died in 1607 and was famous for her fine buildings, her charitable works, and her four husbands!

Top
St Peter's Street, Derby in the mid-1870s showing a large variety of shops with their wares on view.

Centre
The river Derwent at Derby looking towards the cathedral, with the churches of St Alkmund's and its spire (now demolished) and St Mary's and on the extreme right the Old Silk Mill, the first in England, founded by John Lombe.

Bottom
The Market Place and Town Hall at Derby in 1906. The open market later moved to the Morledge and is now, in all its confusing modern form, in the new Eagle Centre. The Town Hall dates from 1842 and replaces the earlier building, which was destroyed by fire.

Of the city's other churches, the memory of St Andrew's, the railwaymen's church, reminds us of provisions made in the nineteenth century for the spiritual and physical welfare of the population in the area around the station and works. A day school opened beside the church site in September 1863, together with a nursery and free evening-classes for adults to learn reading, writing and arithmetic. The church itself was consecrated on Ascension Day 1866 by the Bishop of Lichfield. Midland shareholders contributed to an appeal by Michael Bass, MP for Derby, and it was designed by Sir Gilbert Scott, architect of the St Pancras Midland Grand Hotel.

Derby marks our terminus and the end of a journey of some 128½ miles. Many of the line's former glories have faded, and the mention of the Midland Railway calls to mind only myriad memories of happier golden days now gone for ever. Yet despite this fact, and despite changing times and habits, the old Midland line to London remains with us – at least for the present – and it is hoped that some of this memorable legacy has found expression within the pages of this book.

Top
The top of the Cornmarket, Derby and Victoria Street with cabs and carts very much in evidence. Johnson's watch and jewellery stores has been moved from the location in the photograph at the top of page 142 to the new site seen here; F. W. Woolworth's store is already open.

Bottom
Tailpiece - the last photograph points back the way we have come, as Jubilee class 4-6-0 5608 'Gibraltar' sets off from Derby with a St Pancras-bound express in about 1946.

List of Stations – St Pancras to Derby

Original station name	Distance from St Pancras		Opened for passenger traffic	Closed for passenger traffic
	miles	chains		
St Pancras	0	0	1 October 1868	—
Camden Road	1	17	13 July 1868	1 January 1916
Kentish Town	1	43	13 July 1868	—
Haverstock Hill	2	24	13 July 1868	1 January 1916
Finchley Road (1st station)	★		13 July 1868	3 February 1884
Finchley Road (2nd station)	3	38	3 February 1884	11 July 1927
West End	3	73	1 March 1871	—
Child's Hill & Cricklewood	5	9	2 May 1870	—
Welsh Harp	6	45	2 May 1870	1 July 1903
Hendon	6	76	13 July 1868	—
Mill Hill	9	28	13 July 1868	—
Elstree	12	35	13 July 1868	—
Radlett	15	17	13 July 1868	—
Napsbury	18	10	19 June 1905	14 September 1959
St Albans	19	69	13 July 1868	—
Harpenden	24	50	13 July 1868	—
Chiltern Green (for Luton Hoo)	27	21	13 July 1868	7 April 1952
Luton	30	18	13 July 1868	—
Leagrave	32	61	13 July 1868	—
Harlington (for Toddington)	37	22	13 July 1868	—
Flitwick	40	18	2 May 1870	—
Ampthill	41	61	13 July 1868	4 May 1959
Bedford (1st station)	49	68	1 February 1859	★
Bedford (2nd station)	49	70	9 June 1980	—
Oakley	52	78	7 May 1857	15 September 1958
Sharnbrook	56	53	7 May 1857	2 May 1960
Irchester	62	54	7 May 1857	7 March 1960
Wellingborough	65	4	7 May 1857	—
Finedon	68	18	7 May 1857	2 December 1940
Isham & Burton Latimer	69	27	7 May 1857	20 November 1950
Kettering	72	1	7 May 1857	—
Rushton	75	47	7 May 1857	4 January 1960
Desborough	78	8	7 May 1857	1 January 1968
Market Harborough	82	75	14 September 1885	—
Langton	86	26	★	1 January 1968
Kibworth	88	74	7 May 1857	1 January 1968
Glen	91	44	7 May 1857	18 June 1951
Wigston	95	31	7 May 1857	1 January 1968
Leicester	99	6	1 July 1840	—
Humberstone Road	99	67	★	4 March 1968
Syston	103	63	1 July 1840	4 March 1968
Cossington Gate	★		before 1860	29 September 1873
Sileby	106	47	1 July 1840	4 March 1968
Barrow-on-Soar	108	71	1 July 1840	4 March 1968
Loughborough	111	46	1 July 1840	—
Hathern	114	32	★	1 January 1960
Kegworth	116	28	1 July 1840	4 March 1968
Trent	119	65	1 May 1862	1 January 1968
Sawley Junction	120	28	30 May 1839	—
Breaston (later Sawley)	121	42	30 May 1839	1 December 1930
Draycott	122	29	1 September 1852	14 February 1966
Borrowash (1st station)	★		30 May 1839	1 May 1871
Borrowash (2nd station)	124	54	1 May 1871	14 February 1966
Spondon	125	69	11 November 1839	—
Derby (1st station)	★		4 June 1839	11 May 1840
Derby (2nd station)	128	37	11 May 1840	—

All distances are taken from the official Midland Railway Distance Diagrams, except Bedford 2nd station.
In all cases the dates of opening refer to the first station on the site and the first station name used is the one quoted.
Entries marked thus ★ indicate where information is lacking.